an infinite thing

THE SHORT LIFE OF KYLE MAGINNIS

The title is taken from a poem, translated
from Spanish, that Kyle wrote in seventh grade.
Its full text appears in Appendix H.

PREFACE

This booklet exists because Rev. William H. Stetson, J.C.D., Director of the Catholic Information Center in Washington D.C., urged Kyle's family to create a record of how Kyle "lived his faith." Though its impetus and purpose, may therefore seem one-dimensional, the resulting portrait is not. I could not write about any other aspect of Kyle—his charity, generosity, creativity, industry, humor—without also writing about his profound devotion to God, and his concomitant love of life. The love of God ran through Kyle like a river constantly overflowing its banks, nourishing every feature of his personality. Kyle's life of faith was the core of his being.

After Kyle's death, we received from his friends many hundreds of cards and letters, a book of classmates' remembrances, many poems and two commemorative musical works. The testimonials in this manuscript were excerpted from these materials. I have identified each author only by a number, thus protecting the privacy of each while permitting the reader to identify two or more statements by the same individual. Many tributes are omitted because their terms made it impossible to both protect the author's privacy and disclose his message. Others were omitted because their essence was captured in quoted comments. Finally, I have omitted the physically grandest tribute of all, "In Loving Memory of Kyle Maginnis"—a sunset-themed, sixty-yard mural painted on Walker Wall at Pomona College by Kyle's devoted friends and teachers—because no photograph of it could be satisfactorily reproduced in these pages.

To all who wrote to us of your love for Kyle, Thank You. Every word you wrote, whether it appears in this little book or not, is known to Kyle and will be preserved among his family's most precious heirlooms.

Several of Kyle's friends who talked to him during the last days of his life found that the topic of conversation, for one reason or another, turned to death. In his last weeks, I believe Kyle suspected that his physical condition was grave. His symptoms suggested an incurable form of brain cancer, from which he would likely have died within two years, even had the aneurism not taken his life so suddenly. Basic information about his condition was readily accessible to Kyle via internet. Thus his thoughts, and therefore his conversations, would naturally drift in the direction of eternity.

All of these friends deliver the same report about those conversations. "Kyle was peaceful about death," they say, "very accepting." I know Kyle would like all of us who loved him and miss him so much to feel that way about his death: Peaceful. Very accepting.

Joan Maginnis Washington D.C. September 2004

2015 SUPPLEMENT TO THE PREFACE

This manuscript is being reprinted for the fourth time because, twelve years after Kyle's death, I continue to receive requests for copies. Kyle's family—indeed, everyone who knew Kyle—feels grateful for these requests and most especially for the prospect they raise, that Kyle's memory will inspire others' love of God and of life, which is God's gift.

Fr. Stetson said this in the Homily he delivered at Kyle's funeral:

> ... [W]hy does God cut short the life of a young person like Kyle, a young man whose starry eyes, sense of humor and infectious smile brought a special joy to everyone he met and to every place he went? * * * ... God's plans are not ours. It was precisely Kyle's youthful, starry-eyed infectious love for others that God has transplanted to eternity. Full of promise and already with the excitement of knowledge and the joy of life and love as service and sharing, he has entered eternity. He is eternally young, and as such we shall meet him again.

That is something to celebrate, isn't it! The very same Kyle we loved, untouched by further "Slings and Arrows of outrageous Fortune," will be nearby (smiling, of course) when each of us finally sees the Face of God.

Joan Maginnis Washington D.C. August 2015

table of contents

CHAPTER ONE: kyle's last hours 1

CHAPTER TWO: kyle's life plan 7

CHAPTER THREE: kyle's life as a catholic 9

CHAPTER FOUR: kyle's student life 14

CHAPTER FIVE: kyle as a son 19

CHAPTER SIX: a mother's remembrance 22

appendices

A. July 11, 2003 Letter from Lauren Moore 33

B. Personal Commentaries, March 2003 - May 2004 38

    I.   Kyle as a Catholic 38
    II.   Kyle as Student and Classmate 41
    III. Kyle as Dancer and Athlete 44
    IV.   Kyle as a Friend 46

C. March 29, 2003 Funeral Mass Eulogy by Alvaro DiVicente 50

D. Article by Daniel Driscoll (Pomona '05) 55

E. Article by Pam Noles, Los Angeles Times 60

F. March 13, 2003 Reference Letter by Professor Martha Andresen   In
    Support of Kyle's Application to the Notre Dame Traditio
    Seminar 64

G. April 28, 2003 Pomona Memorial Service Address
    by Richard Cannon 67

H. Phi Beta Kappa Commendation for Kyle Chrysostom Maginnis 70

CHAPTER ONE: *kyle's last hours*

———⁓———

In relating the ways in which Kyle lived his religious Faith, it is appropriate to begin at the end.

A sophomore at Pomona College in southern California, Kyle emailed me in Washington D.C. on Friday morning, March 21, 2003. Arriving at my office desk, I was pleased, but not surprised, to find mail from "Sparkling Chrysostom" in my inbox. Here is what he wrote:

> *Dearest Mother,*
>
> *I have decided to visit the hospital tomorrow to get my headache checked out, as my research indicates I should do. However, I do need my/your insurance information to do so— could you e-mail me everything you might think I'll need to get admitted to the hospital? Thanks so much—I suppose they might? take an MRI or something like that. Does that cost money? Ought I be concerned about avoiding certain tests for financial reasons? Anyway, don't worry about anything. I love you so much!*
>
> *Your son, Kyle Maginnis*

This news of itself was not excessively alarming to Kyle's family. Kyle had mentioned to me previously that he had had headaches, and the family's medical history suggested that cerebral anomalies were not very consequential. Further, given the stresses of the mid-term exams that he had completed the previous week, and the particular pressure of one professor's criticism of Kyle's work, headaches seemed to follow in the normal course of collegiate events. Moreover, since Kyle had returned to campus after Christmas break, his frequent emails home had raised no special alarm.

The next morning however, Kyle phoned and in an amused voice said, "You'll never guess what happened, Mom! I went to the ER last night and they told me I have an 'unidentified cerebral mass,' and put me in ICU—an isolation room, with all kinds of wires hooked up to me!" Kyle offered what little medical information he knew, saying in response to my frank terror at the fact he had been put in ICU, "Don't worry, Mom. Where's that stiff upper lip!" He discouraged me from coming to California—"Don't come yet," he said, "at least not until I get the results from the MRI they've scheduled. I didn't even want to call you until then, but Cindy, the night nurse, told me to call you." He did mention, laughingly, that he'd introduced himself at the ER by telling the admissions clerk that he thought he had a brain tumor. "I think they were kind of irritated with me," he said. And after the CAT scan, the doctor seemed to be vexed with him because "I was not taking the news with sufficient gravity."

"I apologized," he said, "but he still looked annoyed. Do you think I was rude?"

Kyle's neurosurgeon reached my cell phone as Jack and I stood in line together at the airport boarding gate of a flight to Los Angeles. The surgeon announced that the MRI revealed a tumor in the posterior fosse area of Kyle's brain, it was evidently treatable, and Kyle should be brought home promptly for the necessary surgery. "That's what I would do if he were my son," the surgeon told us, "bring him home for surgery."

On arriving at the hospital, I was surprised to learn that Kyle had been moved out of ICU into a semi-private room on the neurology floor. Sitting on the bed nearest the door as I entered that room was a sad-looking, middle-aged man with a long, mean scar across the top of his shaven head. He seemed so self-absorbed, I did not speak to him, but quietly passed him by and then pushed aside the curtains dividing the semi-private room into two segments. There I found a bustling coterie of college students assembled around the window-side bed. On it, beaming, Kyle sat almost upright, an IV strapped to his right forearm, which he held on his chest at an awkward angle.

In his customary lilting voice, effusive of well-being, Kyle greeted me ("Hi Mom!") and instantly commenced introducing me to his eight or ten visitors: "Wait 'till I tell you about my friends!" he began.

Not halfway through what struck me as a conscientious litany of each individual's accomplishments and credentials, Kyle suddenly stopped and said, "No—wait! I'm going too fast. I'll start over." He then returned his attention to the first person in line beside his bed, naming her, reciting from memory and with affectionate care all of her achievements—memorized so thoroughly he could have been reading from her resume. And so he proceeded from one to the next, smiling like a father, as proud of his friends—from water polo medalist to Writing Fellow to valedictorian to debate champion—as he would have been if they were his own children. I was long accustomed to displays of Kyle's remarkable memory, but in this *en masse* introduction, he outdid himself, and reassured me that he surely would recover his health and be OK.

Soon visiting hours ended and the nurse gently sent the classmates away. When the last was gone, Kyle's sunny expression faded and he told me that he felt "so tired; I haven't slept in two days." The IV in his arm was mysteriously painful and awkward. I suggested it be moved to the back of his hand, and he agreed that might help. He also expressed concern because Saturday was his customary day for going to confession. In the ICU, he had asked if a priest would come, and had been expecting one—in vain— throughout the day.

We made plans together for the inevitable surgery. He fretted about missing final exams. Presuming I knew the source of this concern, I said, "Perhaps you don't have to miss graduating with your class. You'll have the surgery right away, recover over spring, and can make up your course work and exams in the summer, and rejoin your class next Fall." Kyle appeared surprised, as if he had not yet considered he might lose his place in the Class of '05. Then he said somewhat wistfully, "I don't think I can do that. You don't realize how competitive it is here." He shook his head, "You don't know how incredibly stressful my life is!" This weary pessimism—so unlike Kyle—struck me as evidence that he was truly ill. "Honey, you don't always need to get A's," I said, and he flashed me that wry and patient smile he sometimes produced in response to the foolish errors of innocents.

We also planned a busy morning—get Kyle discharged, return to his dormitory to pack his things, and try to get to the airport in time to catch a daylight flight home. "I wrote Grandma a letter," he said. "It's on my desk. We have to remember to mail it."

Answering a phone call from his father and sister in Washington, his face again broke into a huge grin and his voice instantly resumed its usual happy tone. "Hi Marcelle! How did the play go?" But the conversation was cut short by another call, this one from the surgeon, and I pressured Kyle to make quick goodbyes. I moved the call to the hallway, to speak privately with the surgeon. "His tumor is operable," he said, "and you can expect a good neurological result." I didn't ask what he meant by "good neurological result," but I cross-examined him briefly about the trip home: Isn't it dangerous? What about the air pressure changes in the plane? The doctor assured me the only immediate threat to Kyle was the danger of swelling, in which case Kyle would be "very sick indeed." But Kyle was being medicated to prevent swelling. It was absolutely safe to take him home.

After talking with the doctor, I was anxious that Kyle be allowed, at last, to sleep. I returned briefly to his room to lend him a favorite cashmere scarf that I was wearing—for him to shelter his eyes from the unforgiving fluorescent glare of the bedside lights—and kissed him goodbye. He smiled again.

Before leaving the hospital, I stopped at the nurses' station and asked if Kyle could have something to help him sleep; they said the doctor had forbidden either sedative or analgesic. "Even an herbal, over-the-counter soporific?" I asked. "Even that," the nurse said. "The orders are to preserve his neurological symptoms." Nor, they told me, would they relocate his IV from his inner forearm to his hand.

Despite having asked the nurses to call me if Kyle's condition changed, I heard nothing from the hospital all night. Up early on Sunday morning, I decided to postpone going Mass until Kyle was discharged. We would go to church together, I thought, then to his dormitory to pack his bags, then head for the airport. I stopped *en route* to the hospital to pick up Kyle's favorite breakfast sandwich from McDonald's.

Arriving on the neurology floor at about 6:30 Sunday morning, I found the door to Kyle's room closed. I waited in the hall, reading the paper, for the patients' breakfast trays to arrive. I assumed he was asleep and did not want to deprive him of a single moment's rest.

Entering his room behind the orderly at 7:30, however, I found him fully awake and in evident distress, his complexion sallow and cool to the touch, his voice strained and weak. "Oh Mom, I've had such a terrible night. My head hurts so much, I haven't slept at all.

"And I've been vomiting . . . but I made sure your scarf was OK." He held up the scarf, smiled slightly, and was seized by another round of vomiting. The orderly matter-of-factly tended to the clean-up, for which Kyle apologized. When orderly left, Kyle said, "Duke helped me during the night, Mom," and gestured toward the man in the next bed. "He was very nice to me, even though I was keeping him up!"

During the next ninety minutes, Kyle's pain and suffering steadily increased, as did my anxiety and confusion: "Is this normal?" I asked myself. "Is this just one of the headaches he has been having? Why aren't the nurses concerned?" My efforts to help Kyle intensified in tandem with Kyle's concern that I not worry and—especially—that I not "bother the nurses; they've been working all night and have so much to do." I had to reassure Kyle that a new shift of nurses was on duty, and that my keeping the nurses apprised of his needs was helpful, not burdensome, to them. He did not seem entirely convinced.

Four times in the next ninety minutes I visited the nurses' station to ask for something to relieve this torment: an icepack, a washcloth, an extra pillow, something—please—for his pain. Around eight o'clock, an assistant dean from the college appeared at the door. By this time, a dreadful anxiety was overtaking me. I grasped his hand and pushed him out into the hall, out of Kyle's earshot: "Find a priest," I said. "Get a priest here right away!"

At one point Kyle said, "It's like a stake being driven through my head." I massaged Kyle's legs to distract his attention. "That feels good, Mom." The nurse said Kyle's doctor had been called, and had ordered another MRI. Kyle by this time seemed to drift back and forth between aware misery and near delirium, thrashing his legs and holding his head in his hands. Twice the nurse refused my request for an injection to alleviate Kyle's pain. An orderly appeared with a wheelchair to take Kyle for the MRI: I stared at him in disbelief. Kyle by this time was writhing in pain and the orderly dumbly realized his expectation that Kyle might get into the chair was ludicrous. The nurse tersely sent the orderly away to get a stretcher.

"Death, pain, death, pain," Kyle said. And, later: "Mom, I'm beginning to be afraid."

I was too frightened to ask what frightened him, and said only, "God is here, Kyle."

I went once again to the nurses' desk and begged the head nurse to do something, "He's asking to die. He's in agony. He says his hands and lips are getting numb!"

Her expression changed, she nodded, picked up a syringe from the desktop and followed me back into his room. "I have something for you, Kyle," she said, "roll over on your side."

Kyle obeyed, and she gave him an injection in his hip. He . . . laughed. "I didn't think anything else could hurt but my head!" With a half-smile, or a grimace, he turned on his back, as if suddenly relaxed. I felt a wave of relief. "Now you'll feel better, Honey," I said, "you'll see." He smiled—or grimaced—again. Seeming oblivious at last to the IV in his forearm, he curled up, weakly pulled the sheet around himself, and closed his sparkling eyes for the last time.

CHAPTER TWO: *kyle's life plan*

Kyle died of a cerebral hemorrhage—an unpredictable complication of a brain tumor. He was twenty years and four months old.

Despite the exhaustion and pain he suffered in the final fifteen hours of his life, despite what I suspect was his dawning realization on Sunday morning that death was near, most of the words Kyle uttered were spoken in praise of, affection for, or concern for others: Me ("Don't worry, Mom! Where's that stiff upper lip?"). The ER physician ("Do you think I was rude?"). His beloved sister and father ("Hi Pop! How's it going? How was the play, Marcelle!"). His visiting classmates and friends ("Lauren is a water polo champion. . . .") The orderly ("I'm sorry about this mess!"); his grandmother ("We have to remember to mail that letter"); his nurses ("Please don't bother them, Mom, they have so much to do!"); his hospital room-mate ("Duke really helped me during the night.").

Kyle expressed more concern that my cashmere scarf receive proper care than that he, himself, did.

By contrast to these numerous concerns, he spoke no word to me expressing concern for his own feelings or health. The fate of his studies troubled Kyle, for his sense of duty in that quarter had always been formidable. But it was I—not he—who personalized the concern by raising the threat of not graduating with his class. As for his shock and worry about his ominous diagnosis? His apprehension at impending major surgery? Fear of possible brain damage? Nothing. Not one word.

This almost-supernatural generosity of spirit—this open heart—was emblematic of Kyle's character throughout life. It was so pronounced, so unusual, yet so consistently natural to him, that he seemed to me to glow, and mysteriously to defy description. This impression certainly did not strike me only after his death, but persisted throughout most of his life. Not two months earlier, for example, I had been visited in my office by a colleague and his college-aged daughter, home for Christmas break. She noticed pictures on my credenza of my three children. I briefly narrated the activities and interests of Vytas and Marcelle but, arriving in turn at Kyle's picture, I fell silent, puzzled. Finally I said, "And this is Kyle. Kyle is . . . different." And left it at that.

Kyle was just shy of five years old when, one night while I was tucking him into bed, he solemnly announced that he had decided what he was going to be when he grew up. "I'm going to be a monk, Mom!"

"Honey, how do you know what a monk is?" So far as I could tell at the time, he had never heard the word spoken and, of course, he could not yet have read it. (His kindergarten teacher later delivered the sober advice that Kyle was "behind his classmates in alphabet.")

"A monk," he announced matter-of-factly, "is a man who gives his life back to God."

Now here, I thought, was a precocious and imaginative mind! We said prayers together, staged the usual boxing match between Kyle and his giant stuffed bear, and exchanged the customary hug and kisses.

I went back downstairs, and Kyle quietly and diligently proceeded to give back to God the remaining sixteen years of his life.

CHAPTER THREE: *kyle's life as a catholic*

Kyle's dedication of his life to God was most obvious in his embrace of Catholicism, and his intense love for God, which manifested itself in an extraordinary open-heartedness toward others. I don't believe a single person who knew Kyle would disagree with this assessment.

God blessed Kyle with a vigorous Catholic upbringing that led him directly and inexorably to truth. To bolster the lukewarm religious training dispensed at his local parochial school, where some Commandments were given even shorter shrift than others, Kyle received catechism lessons through Catholics United for the Faith, and also from two excellent volunteer teachers at St. Mary's parish in downtown Washington D.C. He received First Communion from Father Aldo Petrini at St. Mary's in 1990, where our family attended the nine o'clock Sunday Tridentine Mass. In 1995, he left the parish school and entered fifth grade at The Heights School in Potomac Maryland, where he received religious instruction under the prelature of Opus Dei. He was confirmed in 2000 by James Cardinal Hickey at St. Matthews Cathedral in Washington D.C. After making four Heights-sponsored pilgrimages to Spain and to Rome, where he once had the privilege of personally greeting Pope John Paul II, he graduated from The Heights high school in 2001.

Offered the truth, Kyle picked it up and ran full-force, at top speed. A naturally pious child, Kyle readily and regularly prayed the Rosary, and asked at Christmas and birthdays to be given a new scapular, a religious picture, or a crucifix (the kind with "Jesus on it," he specified) to put on the wall in his room. When we paid summertime visits to his grandparents in Michigan, Kyle attended daily Mass with his grandmother (while I slept), and even stayed after Mass to recite the rosary with my mother and her friends!

Sometime in high school, having attained a modicum of independence, Kyle became a daily Communicant. As others may know, this sort of development in a child can disconcert a household that is shared by even one less devout Catholic. Indeed, for a brief period, Kyle's piety threatened to wax irritating.

Kyle never directly, or even implicitly, chided others for devotional laziness. Nonetheless, his indefatigable weekly Confessions and daily Mass attendance—bicycling miles through rain, sleet, snow—were, well, there all the time. These were non-negotiable practices of the boy. To them were added his particular solemnity during grace at meals, his meticulous Signing of the Cross, his reminding me—his Mother!—to pray the Angelus at noontime and, most unsettling of all, his tendency to genuflect when passing before a crucifix in our home. These provoked, in me at least, reactions sufficiently expressive that Kyle soon tamped down his visible pieties, and settled into an un-imposing devotional regimen that, I believe, he followed faithfully until death.

Judging from written evidence and my personal knowledge, this durable routine went well beyond daily Mass and Communion (he regularly volunteered to assist the priest at Mass and often served as a Eucharistic minister) and weekly Confession. Though Kyle never reported his devotional practices to me, I know from observation and intuition that his routine included, at least, very ample daily prayer—certainly the Angelus and the rosary, as well as frequent, probably daily, meditation. Of course, he also read voraciously of a personal library of theological books so dear to him that he carried great portions of it back and forth across the country in rhythm with Pomona's school calendar. And finally, Kyle made frequent small sacrifices and spiritual resolutions, and practiced personal deprivations. Since he never mentioned these, I only suspected them while he was in high school. But after his death, I discovered hard evidence in the form of numerous, disjointed notes in this or that notebook.

Some examples, which possibly include some un-cited quotations:

> Kyle's *"list of mortifications to preserve Our Lord's great gift to us, His children, our souls: no snacks; no dessert; cold showers; no music, eat something unappetizing at each meal."*

"Lord Jesus Christ, take all my freedom, my memory, my understanding and my will. All that I have and cherish You have given to me. I surrender it all to be guided by You. Your grace and

Your love are wealth enough for me. Give me these, Lord Jesus. I ask for nothing more."

Kyle's "goal at Pomona: Learn to pray—Christ should be absolute first in your life, prayer should go to the deepest layer;" and

"If I am to be alone in this college, let me be with Christ alone. Prayer is always first—everything should be prayer."

Near the time of his high school graduation, at age eighteen, Kyle approached his parents with the not-entirely-surprising news that he had decided to become a numerary of Opus Dei. We asked him to wait a year before taking such a step, and Kyle's father expressed his intuition that marriage and fatherhood were Kyle's true vocation. If Kyle was disappointed at our response, and most particularly at our request that he postpone joining Opus Dei, he did not show it. "Okay," he said, and smiled. But I suspected that our reaction was hard for him to gracefully bear. Similarly, if Kyle discredited his father's vocational advice, he spoke no word against it. Instead, as was later demonstrated, he took that advice to heart and gave what used to be called 'the old college try' to finding a wife.

So far as we believe and evidence suggests, Kyle's devotional observance never flagged during his two years as a student resident at Pomona College, which he entered in August 2001. Moreover, he persisted in the face of two daunting challenges: There was no Opus Dei Center at Pomona; indeed, no organized Catholic presence whatever. And there was no daily Mass celebrated within walking distance of campus. Kyle took immediate action to resolve both problems. He began regularly to take the fifty-mile train trip back and forth through Los Angeles to Tilden Center, the Opus Dei residence on the UCLA campus. And, in short order, Kyle became well-known on campus for borrowing bicycles with which to transport himself to Mass at the nearest church.

Kyle's appalling skill as a bicyclist was legendary, comparable to his notorious driving skill, which had forced his parents to confiscate his driver's license within months of its issuance. It may fairly be said that Kyle's ability to attend daily Mass at Pomona was a gift from any number of extremely patient and generous friends—none of whom, apparently, was even Catholic. One such friend aptly summarized the situation by writing later of Kyle:

> *You enriched my life. Thank you.*
>
> *You brought my bike back to me with pieces in your hands. Not so much thanks for that. (1)*

Throughout his career on Pomona's decidedly—even aggressively—secular campus, Kyle was a faithful disciple of Christ, ready and eager at any moment to share his faith and, if necessary, defend it. The gist of his missionary career is reflected in this note by a fellow student:

> *My most recent interaction with Kyle was for a student religious diversity panel. I remember that we were looking for a practicing Catholic to serve on the panel, and when we asked the Resident Hall Supervisors' staff, the reaction was enormous. Ten people must have almost shouted Kyle's name. (2)*

At one weekday Mass during sophomore year, Kyle at last made the acquaintance of a fellow-Catholic who was a Claremont student. Together they rather bemusedly established Pomona's first Catholic Student Union, an organization whose membership was halved months later by Kyle's death. That fellow-Catholic later wrote of Kyle:

> *In the comments people made about Kyle, so many talked about this smile. It was indeed a great smile—always ear to ear, almost unrealistic. But there were other faces. . . . At Mass, I oftentimes noticed a much graver look about him, coupled with a longing look as he stared at the Tabernacle. His smile muscles certainly got a workout in his lifetime, but when they were at rest, his usual expression was contemplative and slightly concerned. (3)*

This observation fully comports with the documentary evidence found after Kyle's death of his inner, spiritual life: For all the exuberance of his apostolate and the extrovert vibrancy of his personality, Kyle's love of God and relationship with Him to some extent remained sheltered in the deepest, most private recesses of his heart and soul—in a place only God could visit.

CHAPTER FOUR: *kyle's student life*

—◆—

Kyle's Catholic classmate also wrote the following, which sums up how Kyle gave his life as a student "back to God":

> *I remember praying the Sorrowful Mysteries of the Rosary with him one day, and we were at the Crowning of Thorns. We were trying to decide what intention we would pray for. He suggested that we pray that we would have the grace to use our intellectual pursuits to the greater glory of God and glorify Him in our studies. He tried to orient his whole life around the Cross and this included his schoolwork. (3)*

God blessed Kyle generously with intellectual talent: High intelligence, creative imagination, and an uncanny ability to speed-read.

When we took him out of the local parish school after fourth grade, we brought him to an educational counselor for IQ testing. Based on hours of testing, she advised that Kyle was very bright indeed, could succeed at any school, and grow up to be "anything . . . just anything he wants to be".

That same summer, Kyle resolved to win the local public library's Summer Vacation Reading Contest. His strategy was direct: Read a little more than usual. He had long since read—and likely re-read— every book in our bibliophilic household. So, twice—and sometimes thrice—each week, I drove him to the library to drop off and pick up dozens, even scores of books. With each visit, he dutifully logged his completed reading with the library staff. Soon enough, the more vigilant staffers began to eye him suspiciously: Was the boy actually reading all those books? Thereafter, at each visit, a librarian would randomly select two or three of the books Kyle was returning, and ask him to deliver on each an oral book report—which he did, with matter-of-fact thoroughness and his usual smile.

Feeling rather skeptical myself—it seemed impossible that he was reading every word of even the longest books—I soon found occasion personally to test Kyle while driving home with him from one of these library visits. I chose the longest, most challenging book of his latest dropped-off collection: A two- or three-hundred pager entitled something on the order of A Children's Ulysses. "What's the book about?" I asked as we pulled out of the library parking lot. From the backseat, under the weight of the dozen or two fresh tomes that sat on his lap, Kyle launched into a rapid, detailed recitation of a complicated plot involving "ay-chiles" and "penny-lope." I drove a mile or two before realizing that he was referring to Achilles and Penelope—names he'd never heard anyone pronounce. By the time we arrived home, I guessed Kyle to be maybe one-quarter through the tale. He showed no sign of fatigue, waning interest or memory lapse. But it was dark outside and getting near bedtime. I thanked him and said that really was enough. I never questioned his reading comprehension again. (Others did, however, with predictable and invariably amusing results.)

Kyle did win that reading contest, having consumed a total of 420 books. The prize was . . . a candy bar—which the library's Director also presented to every other participant. The award ceremony was frustrating for Kyle's family: Despite hanging construction-paper mobiles with names of each contestant and their number of books read, the library staff refused to give Kyle any special mention or announce any particulars of his achievement. Instead, the Director merely read the name of each contestant in alphabetical order and handed over the candy bar. This frank censorship of his achievement annoyed me deeply, but Kyle didn't seem to mind. When his family broke into wild applause at the eventual, but undistinguished, mention of his name, he laughed with embarrassment.

As a student, Kyle was not a certified genius; he was not even at the top of his Heights class. But he was absolutely driven to achieve as much as possible with the materials at hand—his talents. During high school, this drive may well have been fueled by a determination to do his best for God. But he never said so. I think that, for Kyle, striving was the same as breathing. I believe he recognized the purpose of his life in The Heights' motto: "The Glory of God is a Man Fully Alive, Doing Ordinary Things Extraordinarily Well."

As a practical matter, Kyle's academic diligence was fueled by a resolution he made as a high school sophomore: Gain admission to Princeton. To do so, of course, he needed a plan. He asked his father for books on how to get into "the college of my choice." Soon, he had ingested ten or twelve of these, and had designed a strategy involving about a dozen goals. These included mandates such as: "graduate in top three percent of class;" "score 800 in the SAT;" "earn credit in all available AP courses;" "win national debate title;" "display academic leadership and initiative;" "achieve athletic distinction;" and "diversify extracurricular achievement"—the factor that resulted in Kyle's fascinating adventures as a mostly-mute member of The Heights' A Cappella Choir. He drew a chart of these goals in bold black ink, with empty boxes in the left margin, in which to place check marks as each was achieved.

Within twenty months of conceiving these goals, Kyle systematically had accomplished every one—and Princeton had denied his early application for membership in its Class of 2005. This stunning disappointment surely was devastatingly painful to Kyle, but secretly so. The day Princeton's rejection letter arrived, Kyle's sister was in California undergoing major surgery, and the family's attention was focused on her. Even Kyle's attention: Telling me the news by phone call to the hospital in California, Kyle brushed off my teary remorse. "It's OK, Mom. I don't mind that much. How's Marcelle doing?"

On his return from California to Washington D.C., Jack gave Kyle a list of nine of the nation's top liberal arts colleges and, in January 2001, Kyle dutifully applied to each. Accepted by all but one (Rice University wait-listed him), Kyle chose Pomona at my urging. Pomona was the most academically distinguished of the lot—even more distinguished, judging from the credentials of the entering freshman class, than Princeton. Shortly after arriving on Pomona's campus, Kyle told me by email that, while he had no clue what his major would be, he was determined to graduate at or very near the top of his class. Why? Kyle wanted Jack and me to be invited to a Commencement Weekend event he had heard about—Pomona's President's elegant, exclusive reception for the parents of the very top graduates.

In Pomona's milieu of super-students, Kyle distinguished himself to an extent that, in a work of fiction, would seem implausible. Academically, he became a Graduate Fellowship Candidate in his first semester, achieved "Distinguished Scholar" status in freshman year, and ranked fourth in his class at the time of his death. By the start of sophomore year, he had studied, performed and talked his way into junior- and senior-level classes. Pomona's registrar described Kyle's "perfect 12.0 G.P.A." in his Fall 2002 semester as "truly astonishing," and thought Kyle was probably the only student in Pomona history who earned two A-Pluses in a single semester. (While Pomona utilized the A+ grade, it did not numerically credit it above a simple A, and thus provided no practical incentive for students to achieve the 'plus.') The registrar further stated not only that Kyle's overall G.P.A. was *higher* than that needed to graduate *summa cum laude,* but also that, continuing to perform at the level maintained through his last mid-term exams, Kyle likely would have graduated first in the Class of 2005.

In sports, it was more of the same. Kyle was not only a member of Pomona's Varsity Men's Soccer Team and the Claremont Colleges Ballroom Dance Team, but he also reigned as the Claremont campus' undefeated 5-College Billiards Champion.

In spare moments, Kyle served as a Writing Fellow tutor; Religious Diversity Panelist; billiards instructor; one of three paid "Small Group Evaluators" advising faculty on teaching effectiveness; founder and president of Pomona's Catholic Student Union; contributor to the Pomona Yearbook; and—in response to his parents' plea that he stop volunteering and get a paying job—champion contestant on the television game show, *WinTuition.* In his *spare,* spare time, he searched for other jobs; faithfully and prolifically corresponded with his family and countless friends; applied for financial aid or scholarships, and—in very last weeks of his life, while also studying for mid-term exams— wrote with painstaking care and countless revisions an essay supporting his March 2003 application for Notre Dame's (paid) *Traditio* seminar on the Christianity in the West, "Reconciling Heart and Mind."

Two of Kyle's ambitions were fulfilled after his death. In April 2003, Notre Dame advised Kyle's fellowship adviser that, had Kyle lived, Notre Dame certainly would have selected him as one of the thirteen fellows in the Traditio seminar. And, on May 14, 2004, by an unprecedented, unanimous vote of the membership, Pomona's Phi Beta Kappa Chapter awarded Kyle a posthumous Commendation for Academic Excellence. After the ceremony, Kyle's family was invited to attend a reception the college Dean hosts for all the new PBK-inductees and their parents. This reception was the annual event that caught Kyle's attention as a freshman, to which he dreamed his parents would one day be invited.

CHAPTER FIVE: *kyle as a son*

———⟡———

Kyle lived his Faith as a son through behaviors I now recognize as perfect obedience, but which—as they occurred—I tended to ascribe to an exceedingly gentle and generous disposition, probably inherited from his sweet-natured Grandmother.

It suffices for me to say that being Kyle's mother was a constant, deep, multi-faceted joy. He gave me not one moment's anxiety for his soul, for his goodness, for his love of God or his destiny for Heaven. Not one moment.

But it is so easy to memorialize a child by selectively recounting sweet behaviors that the credibility of a mother's such recitations is impeached by love. Certainly, any recitation by me of Kyle's virtues would be suspect. Why would any loving mother recall a discouraging image of her dead son?

Therefore, I relate here a single, unedited episode of Kyle's later life that I recognize, and believe others would recognize, as emblematic of his character and spirit as a son and a person.

In late summer 2001, a few weeks before Kyle was to start school at Pomona, I asked him to please give his room a thorough cleaning, making it suitable for overnight guest stays. Having in mind nothing more than refreshed bed linens, a cleared desktop and neatened clothes closet, I said, "just make it pleasant for company, in case someone should visit." He said, "Sure, Mom. But where should I put my stuff?" I commissioned him the use of a neglected upstairs closet.

Day after busy day passed, but the task remained un-done. I was more curious than apprehensive on this account; Kyle always did what I asked (or even hinted). He always kept his promises. Nonetheless, when the rest of the family went to bed the night before his flight to LA, the *status quo* prevailed in Kyle's room.

I rose early the next morning to find Kyle's bags, neatly packed, waiting at the front door, Kyle dressed and ready, and his bedroom virtually stripped. All the wall posters, religious art works, friends' photographs, sports trophies, chess paraphernalia, school notebooks and study materials, model cars, ancient lego sculptures, debate medals, firecrackers, sling shot, baseball bat, and any number of other boyish mementos had vanished from the room. The crucifix missing; the desk swept clean; his bookcases emptied; his clothes, art supplies, radio clock, calligraphy materials—everything—gone. It had all been packed with ingenious economy into the hall closet. The sight of his barren room broke my heart and filled me with a premonition that he would never come home again. "I didn't mean this, Kyle," I said in a small voice. "It's still your room!" But there was no going back; it was time to leave for the airport.

This incident illustrates Kyle's willingness, in honoring and obeying his parents—thus, in doing what he perceived to be God's will—to erase himself. Not only that, but to do so with no sense of injury, or even mild surprise. To Kyle, the fourteen years of life he had spent and memorialized in that bedroom naturally were less important than my casual wish for pristine guest quarters.

Kyle likewise had obeyed us without question or complaint in Fall of 1999 when, after he totaled his first car and—weeks later—received a $450 ticket for recklessly driving his second car, we took away his driving privileges. Not once in the remainder of his life—through countless rainy or freezing bike trips to and from Church, tedious metro rides to visit far-flung suburban friends, awkward dates conducted on foot or via public transportation—did Kyle complain that we would not let him drive.

Likewise he obeyed when we asked him to postpone becoming a numerary for one year; when in January 2000 we asked him to take time during his Christmas break to complete applications to nine colleges; in 2001 to choose Pomona; in Spring 2002 to forego doing any more unpaid volunteer work; in Fall that year, to get a paying job and make some money; and in March 2003, though he was painfully, frighteningly ill, to write a cheering letter to his Grandmother (a letter in which, true to form, he expressed his hope to "establish some kind of regular correspondence" with her).

And so on.

At Kyle's wake, one of the scores of parents in attendance who had known Kyle very well for a number of years approached me and said ten words that I will always cherish for their generosity: "I have an imperfect son," she said. "You had a perfect son."

CHAPTER SIX: *a mother's remembrance*

Mothers supposedly know their children best. How did I know Kyle?

When Pam Noles, a reporter for the local newspaper, asked me several times to say something for the article she was writing about Kyle, I repeatedly put her off. It was April 2003—too soon after his sudden death to think clearly or objectively about my son, much less talk about him to a stranger. But a photographic image appeared again and again before my eyes, and I eventually described it to Pam: Kyle, aged eight or ten, perched on the roof of our friends' house-under-construction in the Russian River Valley, tennis-shoed feet swinging playfully off the edge of the sloping roof tiles. The sun was setting behind him; the photographer on the ground before him. The image of his face—smiling, of course—was half-lost in the light of the sun.

He was there, yet not there—at the same time. That is how I knew Kyle.

This sense I had—of an evanescent Kyle—was almost immediate. He'd taken a nasty battering with a difficult birth. Arriving black-and-blue, with a topsy-turvied blood picture, and spiking a fever at age two days, the doctor isolated him from me for several days. And there were other problems that diminished for him the most routine of infant comforts. Yet he was a perfectly placid child, entirely content in the world, not because it was perfectly comfortable—it wasn't—but for some other reason. As the mother of any such baby can testify, this is a marvelous and mystifying thing to behold.

Yet Kyle did not lead a placid life! It's hard to count the cataclysms that befell him, the times I marveled that he had escaped alive and unhurt from this or that catastrophe. Even before he displayed in maturity his characteristic, maddeningly cheerful recklessness, Kyle seemed to be falling continually into the circumstantial traps of whimsical, dangerous Fate.

There was the stroller mishap with a tour bus when he was ten months old; the horrific car crash at age thirty months; the aborted dog-attack; that bizarre post-storm pilgrimage through the downed electric wires at four years; the runaway big-wheel accident at age five, when he crashed into a brick wall (choosing, wisely, to hit the wall rather than cross the road ahead, with swirling creek just beyond) whence he was instantly rescued by passing D.C. Police officers (he thought they were taking him to jail!); his backward fall on the glass coffee table—shattering it; that terrifying, nighttime, downhill three-wheeler adventure in a major snow storm, when only my screams spared him a front-end collision with an SUV whose driver could not see Kyle through the blizzard.

When he was eleven, I wrote a poem—or, rather, a poem turned up on the page as I wrote—that seemed to predict his death.

> *The school bus stops at the curb of time*
> *And opens jealous doors.*
> *But the air has memorized his springing form*
> *And beams it back to me . . .*
> *He's gone! He's gone!*

I tried to change the words, because they frightened me. But the words would not be changed.

Then there was Kyle's impenetrable ignorance of time. Many people noticed this amusing gap in Kyle's otherwise firm grasp of theoretical science. Living with it, however, was not invariably funny. It fell to his twin brother Vytas to pick up lots of the slack left by Kyle's disconnect with the Clock of Life. Vytas carried the heavy load, but we all got used to it. Once, however, it forced upon me a startling sense of Kyle's "otherness."

One Indian summer evening, Kyle and I were sitting on the back porch, chatting after dinner. He was sixteen or seventeen. He'd brought home a question from school, regarding an event scheduled in February. "How far from now is that, exactly?" he asked.

"You know—February," I said. "That month after January." His face betrayed not a shred of understanding. My brow surely furrowed as I ventured, "About four months from now." He nodded cooperatively, but that quizzical look never left his face. "After Christmas and New Years' . . . ?" I ventured, hopefully. No reaction.

I asked him to recite the months. He began, "October. February." Thoughtful pause. "May." I stared, stunned and silent. "November, August . . . "

"Don't you know them in order, Honey?" I asked.

"No."

"Wait here."

Moving "as if in a dream," I sped into the kitchen, then returned to sit down next to him with pen and paper in hand. I drew an oval, suggesting that he visualize the year as a circle with the four seasons on opposing sides—which I helpfully illustrated with symbols (sun, snowman, etc.). I divided the circle into twelve sections, and labeled each as one month. Kyle pondered the diagram with slightly pursed lips. "Thanks, Mom!" he grinned at me. "This is great." Later, he took the paper up to his room, no doubt for further study.

As I've noted, Kyle's loose association with reality had physical as well as temporal aspects. For example, within six days of receiving the gift of his grandparents' trusty Oldsmobile, Kyle totaled it. We already knew that Kyle had some 'challenges' in this quarter, and had advised that he always let Vytas drive when they were together. But, one night, their tandem plans when awry, and Kyle drove off into the rainy night alone. With only the vaguest grasp of his location, and thinking he was entering a freeway entrance ramp, Kyle took an exit ramp at high speed. He flew so fast off the curve that the car went airborne, back seat driver's side smashing laterally into one tree, and front seat passenger side on the ricochet into another. Kyle told me he emerged from the wreck through a shattered window: untouched, perplexed, contrite—and laughing to be still alive.

Within weeks, behind the wheel of a new—even heavier—car, he caught official police department notice by executing a grotesquely ill-conceived U-turn in downtown, rush-hour Bethesda. The driving game was up.

Yet, even on a bicycle, the boy was in constant danger for his life. He could not or would not heed the practical rules of physics. One episode at Pomona in freshman year had his friends—his beloved, faithful, patient friends—driving him to the Emergency Room so doctors could scour the festering gravel out of Kyle's hands and arms, mementoes of a miscalculated turn taken on a borrowed racing bike at too-high speed because he was late to cheer Pomona's team at some sports event. (As recounted in Appendix A, *infra,* Kyle's friends took him to the hospital again at the very close of his life—an act of love that is the sole reason why I was able to be with Kyle when he died.)

Then there was his extraordinary departure from home for Pomona after Christmas break in January 2003. As the date approached, I'd been feeling especially sad and apprehensive, and took care to bring with me a camera for last-minute picture-taking at the airport. Instead—as recounted in Pam Noles' article for the Los Angeles Times—Kyle's family spent the time trying desperately to identify which plane he was supposed to board (Kyle having assumed that I would know!). The rush slowed only as Kyle was disappearing into the airport security line and his family was drifting away down the hall toward the parking lot. Teary, I looked back, wishing I could have taken at least one photograph, but annoyed with myself for romanticizing this routine return to college. Tall Kyle, barely visible in the distance, opening his carry-on bag for the screener, turned toward me and . . . smiled.

A distinct, hard idea burst upon my mind: I would never see him again. I waved and smiled back at him, turned and followed my family down the bright corridor. I scolded myself for indulging melodrama and drove home, meditating on the statistical safety of air travel.

When I replay in my mind this airport scene, I study the images—visual and emotional—as if through a magnifying glass, and I wonder if my dread was not so much that I would never see Kyle again, as that Kyle would die. The latter idea so blends with the first, how could I separate them in my mind? And then I study still older memories, and realize that I have experienced that same apprehension before, at any number of inconsequential goodbyes, like seeing him off at the school bus stop. To a greater or lesser extent, wasn't I always imagining that we would lose him? Not because his death was always just around the corner. But because Kyle seemed perpetually and dangerously closer to eternity than the rest of us?

I do not know the spiritual significance of Kyle's other-worldly traits, his curious amusement at life, his eerily indiscriminate love for people. While uncommonly (at least in my experience) encountered to the degree manifest in Kyle, they certainly are not unknown among men. Nor, certainly, do I know the significance of the vivid sense I've had all these years—of Kyle here, yet not here. Or why that image of Kyle smiling from the rooftop reflects, to me, a truism about his soul.

But I believe that Kyle's behavior and personality, and my emphatic impression of him, reflected a simple reality: Kyle lived his life on earth with one foot in eternity. It was as if he had made, at birth, an incomplete transition into this material world from being an idea in the mind of God.

For Kyle, therefore, going home to God was not that long a trip.

Kyle was different that way.

Rehobeth Beach DE August 1988

Chevy Chase MD May 1997
(with Vytas and Marcelle)

Porter-Bass Vineyards, Russian River Valley, CA
July 1998 (with Vytas)

Camino de Santiago, Spain January 1999
(with Heights classmates)

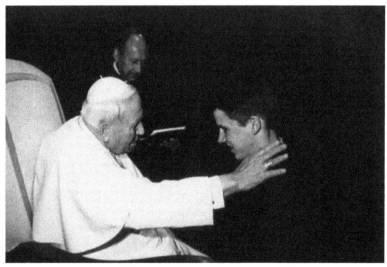

With Pope John Paul II Vatican City April 2000

Potomac MD Fall 2000 (with Vytas)

At Home in Washington D.C. 2002 (with Marcelle and Posy)

Idyllwild CA February 2003

APPENDICES

—ʍ—

A. July 11, 2003 Correspondence from Lauren Moore

What follows is the text of an email written in response to questions that Kyle's family raised regarding how Kyle finally came to be at the hospital on March 21. Like the writer, other persons named here were also his good friends and members of Pomona's Class of 2005.

Dear Mrs. Maginnis,

. . . [I]t has been very difficult for me to sit down and write a letter to you about Kyle. I have been thinking of writing to you every day, but I've been making excuses to avoid doing so because it means I have to think about a friend that I miss so dearly. * * *

I don't really know where to start. I have so many thoughts about Kyle running through my head every day. I will try to recount the last few days I spent time with Kyle as well as I can. Like Rich [Cannon], I was not on campus for the whole week of spring break. I came back to school on March 19 because I had to be at water polo practice the next day at noon. Kyle, Sarah [Sperry] and I went out to dinner at Hero's, a local restaurant with gigantic portions and huge glasses of lemonade. Kyle and I split an order of potato skins, which is an appetizer, and we could not even get through half of them. We debated about friendship and whether or not it was a selfish relationship. After I made a comment about the artist Jackson Pollock, and Kyle had never heard of him, we decided that we complete each other very well because I know about art history, and he knows about everything else.

Afterwards, the three of us rented "Monsoon Wedding," and drove to the grocery store, and bought three cartons of ice cream. This was the first time Kyle mentioned his headaches to me, but he brushed it off as "no big deal" as he often tended to do with issues related to himself. When we were walking through the parking lot, however, he stumbled, and attributed this to his headache. Sarah mentioned taking him to the doctor, and I agreed, but Kyle said it was no big deal at all and changed the subject.

The next day, Thursday [March 20, 2003], Kyle still had a headache. Rich was back at school at this point, and mentioned that Kyle had complained of headaches earlier than this week, as well. The three of us told Kyle we were taking him to the hospital, but he didn't have his insurance information. We decided he would email you, and that we would take him on Friday. Kyle mentioned that he had researched brain tumors and their symptoms, and had been paying close attention to where in his head he had been in pain. He continued, though, to try to change the subject and make excuses for why he didn't want us to take him to the hospital, but that's just Kyle's way of being polite. He is as stubborn as they come, too, and was still protesting the next day when we actually drove to Pomona Valley Hospital. Sarah and I brought reading and knitting, and Kyle settled in to the crowded ER waiting area while Sarah and I waited outside where there was room.

A couple of hours later, Kyle was all set to leave because he hadn't been called and did not want to make Sarah and I wait any longer. We of course refused to take him home, and joined him in the waiting room. Kyle began to read a beauty magazine that Sarah had brought along. He came to a perfume advertisement and tried to gracefully peel it open to sample it, and instead tore the entire page out. He quietly tucked the paper away in the magazine and turned the page when a woman across the room exclaimed, "you're not even going to smell it, after all that!?" Kyle smiled and offered the woman a sniff of the perfume advertisement, as well. As usual, Kyle was making friends with everyone.

After a brief, heated argument with Sarah over the war and the evening news, Kyle insisted again that we leave. I had a game early the next day and Sarah was looking tired, so we decided to leave Kyle with Sarah's cell phone and I made Kyle promise he would not give up until he was seen by a doctor, and to call me when he had been seen so that I could pick him up. He told me he would call me by 2 a.m. if he had not been seen, just to let me know. I believe it was about 11:30 when we left him.

I dropped Sarah off at her room and went to visit another friend. I talked to him for a while, before he walked me home and told me to get some sleep before my game. Just as I was climbing into bed, Kyle called. He told me he had been seen, and that the doctors found something in his head.

"They want me to stay overnight just to keep me under observation. I don't want you freaking out on me, focus on your game tomorrow and don't worry a minute about me. This is just a precaution. It's usually nothing. Don't worry, Lauren!" I remember him sounding so calm and more concerned about me and Sarah and Rich than himself. I also remember him joking about a brain tumor, but not saying anything serious about actually having one. He told me he would call me on Saturday to let me know what was going on.

On Saturday, in between my games, I picked up a message from Kyle giving me his ICU phone number and telling me that he had a brain tumor. He laughed about it, saying, "I guess this is why it's a good thing we have all these smart Pomona students studying to become doctors!" He wanted me to come check him out of the hospital so we could hang out around school. He said, quite jokingly, if he was going to die, he'd rather spend his last moments on campus instead of in a cold, sterile hospital. He ended the message saying he'd better go because the nurse was about to take Sarah's phone from him so he'd better stop making so much noise. . . .

After the games, Rich, Sarah and I drove to the hospital to visit Kyle. He said he had gotten in touch with you, and that you were going to get to the hospital hopefully around 8 p.m. Kyle spend most of the time that we were there trying to convince us to check him out of the hospital. He thought if he was going to be flown back home anyways for the surgery, he might as well leave right now. We told him he should wait for you to arrive before doing anything. He kept trying to change our minds. Finally, Sarah asked Kyle to at least get the doctor's opinion, which he did. Everyone advised against his leaving. He then wanted to sneak out, and threatened to pull out the IV in his arm a number of times. Eventually he mentioned that he felt nauseous, and called a nurse in to give him medication to make him feel better. He of course chatted with every nurse, every staff member, smiling and charming people left and right, always talking with people on a first name basis. We kept trying to change the subject so that Kyle would stop asking us to take him out of the hospital. Kyle was cheerful through, and managed to get in touch with Mr. Maginnis by phone. A couple of other students topped in to say hello to Kyle. That is when you arrived, and we said our goodbyes, hoping to see him again soon.

I guess that was all a very roundabout way of answering your questions. Kyle was refusing the entire time to go to the doctor, being his wonderfully stubborn self, because he didn't want to inconvenience anyone. When we finally told him he was going, he reluctantly went, but only if we promised it wasn't an issue (which, of course, it wasn't). I had no idea that Kyle had assumed it was as bad as it was. I thought the entire time Kyle thought it was no big deal. Even when he was diagnosed with the tumor, he spent so much time reassuring all of us that it wasn't going to be a big deal, and that he was a healthy, strong young man who would pull through better than anyone else he knew.

Sarah and Rich were so strong through everything that happened. We have all become closer and I can feel Kyle in us whenever we are all hanging out, eating, laughing, or having a heated debate about anything. We all tell funny stories about him, of course, often relating to him losing a bike or telling a corny joke that always made me laugh with him and everyone else laugh at us: "I'm so tired, Goodyear should sponsor me!" That was one of my favorites.

He'd also grab me as we were walking home after a meal in the dining hall and teach me a dance step or two, always knowing I would have two left feet, yet still dancing me through everything with such grace.

I remember one night; everyone in the "tower" (as we affectionately call where Rich, Alex, Dave, Kyle and Will lived last year) was up late studying and writing papers. I was done with work so I had everyone write down what they wanted from the Starbucks in the village. I ordered for myself and politely presented the list to the cashier so that she could ring up what everyone else wanted, and she smiled as she read it. Kyle had written, "Caramel Apple Cider big size if they have it, thank you, I love you!" I laughed as she pointed it out to me.

Recently, while on vacation with my family, I was flipping through television channels. I came across the Game Show Network and thought I leave it there in case "WinTuition" came on. It's a habit I've developed since Kyle was on it, because it reminds me of the ridiculous and wonderful stories that Kyle told us about his experience on the show. When the program lineup appeared onscreen, WinTuition was indeed about to start! I laughed and sat down to watch and to my amazement, Kyle appeared. I didn't move an inch as I watched him smile and joke his way through the episode. I could not believe that at that random time, when I unexpectedly had the television on, Kyle was on. When I think back on it, I know it was not a coincidence. Everything worked out because someone had really wanted me to see Kyle again.

I hope that this letter has helped you somehow.

Love,

Lauren Moore

B. Personal Commentaries, March 2003 - May 2004

The following excerpts are taken from notes, letters and essays written by Kyle's teachers, counselors and friends shortly after his death. With only two exceptions (in which excerpts from quotes from the same person appear under different headings), each paragraph contains the thoughts of a different author, each of whom is designated by a number. For the sake of their privacy, a few alterations of the original texts were made to delete identifying references to the author, or to persons other than Kyle.

I. Kyle as a Catholic:

Kyle stood out as a pillar of faith and commitment, one who preached and practiced the highest forms of devotion. His daily religious activity was astounding and inspiring. . . . At the same time, he seemed to me a wonderfully humble servant, one who was looking upward and inward in his every thought and action, not outward for the praise of others. I know from other settings that he was a scholar and a gentleman, but for me he will always stand out as a man of faith and of God. (2)

Kyle had a faith and deep love for Jesus that was incredible. In everything he did, his love for God shined through. Even though he felt the lack of other Catholics on our campus, he never compromised his faith or devotion to God. In all the time that I knew him I was [impressed] and encouraged by his faith and boldness and even now it makes me want to follow his example. (5)

When I think of Kyle, the thought that comes to mind is: "Well done, my good and faithful servant." (6)

Kyle is one of the most remarkable young men I have ever known. I felt honored to have been able to know him and learn from him. He is what every parent should dream for. He brings so much good into the world through his wit, his loyalty, his intelligence and his piety. And in a very special way, through his kind heartedness. I was able to witness that on more than one occasion, and it impressed me profoundly. Kyle had a knack for lifting up the 'little guy,' and making him feel like a million bucks. His optimism and zest for life was contagious. And he clearly had a great rapport and prestige with his friends. A real leader, who brought God into the lives of those around him in such a cheerful and natural way. Over these days, many conversations I've had with Kyle have come to mind. They make me laugh, and they make me ponder. I thank God for blessing me with Kyle's friendship. He helps me strive to be a better priest. His life sets the standard very high. . . . But I know he is up there helping me along, with that generous heart . . . and that beaming smile. (7)

. . . Kyle was an answer to my fervent prayer that [my daughter] would meet a Christian friend [at Pomona College] whom she could respect. Kyle was the answer. [My daughter] . . . never found a faith that worked for her . . . [so much] just blocked her vision. Kyle broke through! (49)

There was a moment today, after the Mass for Kyle at the Cistercian Abbey, that Kyle's presence—not just a memory—was so strong and happy that I couldn't help from smiling, laughing and starting to cry at the same time. It was just brief, as if he were poking his head in the door to say he is OK, passing on his smile, then off again. I look forward with you, to when we meet him again, and until then I will try my best to follow his example, trying cheerfully to get there. (8)

Kyle's emails always made me laugh out loud, and they also inspired me when he'd write about the Faith or his desire to help those who'd fallen away from the Church. It had been wonderful, too, to see his devotion and love for our Lord during the England trip. Kyle never pushed the Faith on anyone, but his incredible faith was evident in all his actions and speech, and it made me want to be like him. Through his charity and care for others, Kyle set an amazing example. His ability to laugh at himself showed his humility and made us all like him even more. He always put everyone at ease and made everyone feel like his best friend. (9)

Kyle was the closest person to Jesus I have ever met. Every person I met through Kyle, and every moment with him, has made my life better. (10)

Kyle was a Kiss from God. Once, because he was joining our family on an early-morning trip to the beach, he spent the night here. In the morning I said, "Kyle would you get a piece of that poster board in the garage and use this duct tape to deflect the water from the damaged window while we're away?" Big smile— "Sure, I can do that!" As we drove away, I glanced back and saw large, bold headlines from the Catholic Register Poster. I am sure my Jewish neighbors were impressed. Kyle left such a trail of laughter. (11)

Kyle was without a doubt the . . . most kind-hearted person I have ever met. Even tonight (March 23, 2003), I was blown away by the number of people who shared some type of relationship with this remarkable man. Believe me, he did stand out. (12)

I met Kyle about a month ago in the campus training room. He was with a few other people, but made it a point to get my name and engage me in the conversation. After that, he said hi to me wherever our paths crossed on campus. That alone was touching to me. . . . After that day, he spoke to me as if we'd known each other for years. * * * After he died, I was shocked, saddened, and angry. My faith in God, while longstanding, is still weak and full of questions. "Why," I asked, "would God take such a wonderful, vibrant, loving person away from us?" Yet, even after his death, Kyle influenced me. His faith was incredibly strong, and I know that he would not question or doubt God's decision. * * * Kyle's life, death, and faith have all strengthened my own faith, and I aspire to be as he was—all of God's love for every person. (13)

His passing has not been the easiest thing. The day he died I went to Mass and wanted to tell Kyle that I had lost one of my dearest and best friends and wanted to talk to him about that. Unfortunately, he was that friend. However, had he been there, Kyle would remind me of that Catholic belief in the Communion of Saints, and that all those who love Christ are united to one another through Him. * * * Of all my friends, I think that Kyle had the greatest chance of making it through the Pearly Gates "as is." His love of Christ has been a great consolation to me. . . . (3)

Of all the people that I knew, I thought Kyle would deserve a miracle— there were so many accidents that he managed to scrape through, I thought that he surely doesn't deserve [to die so young]. I thought that since he was such a fun loving, alive, young, intelligent, caring person somehow this wouldn't be true. I can't grasp it. It's horrible. Horrible. ***
So athletic, happy, energetic, friendly, funny, he loved to teach and he was good at it. Ambitious, loving, genuine, sincere, he was "all there." Kyle would give you all of his attention, really be with you, focus on who you were, what was wonderful about you. His smile—I hardly ever say Kyle when he wasn't smiling . . . his grin would be just there, the one dimple in his cheek, his mussed-up hair, his loud voice telling his hilarious stories . . . it's all so unreal. I happened so fast. How come I didn't understand that I needed to say goodbye? *** Always reaching out, crossing invisible lines of social rules in order to touch someone who hadn't expected him to notice

them. Such intensity, such a strong light. He shone everyday. Kyle inspires me to grasp life with all my heart and love what I have been given. (60)

II. Kyle as Student and Classmate

Our entire campus is grieving; we cannot reconcile the idea that our dear friend, who truly seemed to be friends with everybody, could really be gone. * * * Kyle carried an infectious fire inside of him. I always looked forward to events where I knew I would see him, be it a writing fellows meeting, a Shakespeare rehearsal, or an impromptu dance session in the lounge, because he never failed to delight me and bring a smile to my face. * * * I am not a religious person, but I know I will remember him as an angel walking among us. (51)

Pomona College is a noticeably better place because of [Kyle]. (29)

Teachers aren't supposed to have favorites, but of course they do. When a student like Kyle comes along, you can't ignore it. He had genuine charisma, you have to call it that—beauty, spirit, intelligence—it was all there. Funny, impish, so smart, with a rare quality about him of, there's no better word for it, goodness—I looked forward to the class because of his presence in it. He lifted it into a special place in my memory . . . When I think of Kyle, I can think of no one more alive, a young life more intensely and joyously lived. It is nearly impossible not think of him in this way. (14)

Kyle . . . was the soul and spirit of the class [that I taught]. (15)

Kyle was a very deep thinker. . . . He put a great deal of thought into the big picture issues. Kyle's educational tenacity could not be divorced from his faith. In all his studying, I think that he was searching for the Truth. (3)

Kyle was the heart of our Shakespeare class. (16)

Kyle was enrolled in [the] . . . class [I taught] this term. I was just getting to know [him,] and to appreciate the truly remarkable person he was. I would ask for one page, Kyle would write four. His last paper . . . was a work of extraordinary quality, quite simply the best in the class. Kyle has been a catalyst for the class—quick to jump in, always remaining after the bell to continue the discussion. I have rarely met a person of his age of such integrity, and for whom the life of the mind and the spirit mattered so terribly much. Nor have I often encountered a student who meant so much to his peers. They realize, as do [his professors], what a privilege it has been to have him among us. (17)

Kyle was . . . without question the most friendly, caring and upstanding person I knew. I never saw him when it didn't brighten my day, and I never left his presence without feeling better than I did before. . . .

I always admired the way he met people and went right into vivid conversation with them. He never judged anyone, and he wanted to be friends with everyone. Kyle was never satisfied with just doing something—everything he did had to be bigger and better than what was asked of him. . . . Kyle never just did anything. I really admired him for that. More than just admiring him though, I loved Kyle. I felt like I was a better person around him. Whenever I doubted myself, he told me that I was doing a good job, and I believed him. He was the best storyteller I have ever met, and he brought me to tears with laughter on many occasions. I loved being around him and sharing in his passion for life. One day, after discovering that we had the same color eyes, we decided that we should go somewhere and introduce ourselves . . . as brother and sister. Mostly it was just a fun idea, but I secretly wished that he really was my brother. I wanted to be friends with him forever, because after meeting Kyle, I couldn't imagine life without him. Sadly, that was not to be, and now I am finding out what life without him is like. It strikes me every day when I see something that reminds me of him—I walk past Harwood and expect to see him skipping out the door, with his dance shoes in a little mesh bag and a huge grin on his face. I walk down the street and see a biker whiz past and my first thought is that it's Kyle, rushing to experience the next amazing thing that life has to offer him. I put on the visor he won in a pool tournament last semester and remember how radiant he was that night, and how on that day I learned how a hero looked. I see the sunset and remember the time I walked to church with him as the sky turned orange and red, and the world was still, and peaceful, and complete. (18)

Kyle . . . is the reason I passed statistics class, he helped me through without complaining, without looking for better things to do. (19)

One of the things I liked most about Kyle was that he could argue really well. It was always so great to have someone to debate with for hours on end—especially since he usually employed diagrams, published works, and the opinions of unwitting strangers. What I liked so much was that we could completely disagree and rip the others' perspective to shreds, but it never became personal. I never felt attacked or upset. I also loved Kyle's almost ridiculous willingness to try new things or learn. Yet even though he was unusually very put together and quick-witted, some of the best memories I have is when a little glimmer of ineptitude would come out. We made pumpkin pie over Thanksgiving break and we had to start over probably three times because Kyle kept forgetting how much of each spice he had put in the bowl as he was measuring. Or when he told me the numerous reasons why he absolutely was not allowed to drive. It always seemed so funny to me that someone who could [defeat] me in an argument and write an amazing Shakespeare paper, could also crash his car—a lot—and mis-measure pie spices. . . . [W]ith the potential to be overwhelming with . . . charisma or intelligence, he had all these little Kyle quirks that made him approachable, and genuine, and real. He was just such a real person despite his rather unreal personality. (20)

My first impression of Kyle (constant smile, booming voice) was that he would make a good game show host. However, as I continued to talk to him and get to know him better, I realized what an interesting and good-natured person he was, aside from his friendly exterior. Kyle was able to joke, talk, and connect with anyone. I introduced him to my younger sister who visited about a month ago, and he wrote her a Valentine on the spot. (21)

There are no words that can bring the sound of Kyle's voice to the world. But the words he has spoken will remain forever embedded in the hearts of all he touched. Kyle is an amazing person with the power to influence so many lives, to help form so many dreams. I wish my words could do justice to his. His memory makes me smile, makes me want to be a better person. He will always be behind me to push me further, just as he would have done to himself. [Kyle] is a blessing to this world. (48)

[Kyle] was a vibrant, charismatic, faith-filled, hope-filled, positive, loving, energetic and energizing young, handsome man who, in a short time, was and is a timeless poster child for God's mission and Pomona's calling as a liberal arts educator. . . . (22, 23)

It wasn't until this year, when we were Writing Fellows together, that I began to know Kyle better. He was one of the warmest, funniest, [most] cheerful people I have ever known. He and I would try occasionally to work together in the Teaching and Learning Center. On March 13, the Thursday before spring break, we were doing that and no one came in for help, so the two of us just talked. We started out discussing an English paper of Kyle's that he was taking a very experimental approach with, but the conversation quickly progressed to a discussion of literary theory, human nature, and the production of knowledge. I think we spent the whole two hours like that. When I got back to my dorm, I told a friend that I had just had one of the most engaging intellectual conversations of my life. I will always remember and treasure it, and my memory of Kyle. Even in the brief amounts of time we spent together, he enriched my life. (24)

I always thought of Kyle as a sort of "Mr. Pomona." [In] his involvement in so many activities and his ability to achieve at them, [he] stood out like no other student. I remember dancing with him in my Latin Dance class and feeling awe at how a freshman could so quickly master techniques that appeared to take years for the more senior members of the team to perfect. When I saw that he was a Writing Fellow this year, I couldn't imagine how any sophomore could be so advanced in that skill to mentor other students. I felt this way until I listened to his comments during our Shakespeare class and marveled at his insight and maturity of thought. His eloquence was unmatched and he truly stood out as an incredible talented individual. (25)

When Kyle interviewed for the [Writing Fellow] position last September— and he clearly wanted the job—he impressed me with his sincere commitment to helping others. Unlike many young people, who disdain showing any exuberance for a cause, Kyle threw himself whole heartedly into his new responsibility. He never missed a meeting, offered good ideas for improving our program, and always exhibited an excellent sense of humor. I can't tell you how much we'll miss him. He stood out as a person who would have tried with all his heart to improve this troubled world. (26)

III. Kyle as Dancer and Athlete

I mostly knew Kyle through soccer. I was a sophomore when he came to preseason practice as a freshman. In inter-squad scrimmages he usually played on the midfield or as a stopper on the reserves squad, so I, as a central midfielder, was often on the wrong side of his fearless tackles and his deceptively effective dribbles. He did not get much playing time that year, but Kyle was one of the few freshmen I've seen who had the courage/madness/audacity to go after anybody and everybody on the pitch. He simply would not back down from a challenge with an onrushing attacker. Not even, I might add, when we were practicing free kicks and he was the "gunner" on the end of the wall. I gave Ian a bad little pass for the shot, and sure enough, Kyle came flying off the end of the wall and nearly deflated the ball...and Ian's leg. No damage done, and Kyle was immediately yanking Ian to his feet with that trademark goofy grin. But for all his fire and determination as an opponent on the training ground, he was always supportive as a teammate. No matter the result of the game or how little time he had been on the field, Kyle would always be there on the sideline at the end of the match, congratulating me on a "great game, great effort, great job...." Even if I had bungled the ball that led to the losing goal. I will always have an image of Kyle helping me and other players to their feet after an early-season loss. Not many of us have the confidence or presence of mind as freshmen to reach out to older players and to help bring the group back together after a tough setback, [but Kyle did]. (27)

It was one of the easiest goals I ever scored. What a perfect ball you played from the right wing! It practically landed on my head! (28)

So I would always make Kyle dance with me. I had a good 25 pounds on Kyle, and I always wanted to be dipped. Every once in a while, I would take Kyle down with me in my super-uncoordinated fashion, but he would still always want to dance with me. (29)

. . . [W]hen I first met Kyle, I thought he was a phony. It hadn't occurred to me that a person could be that friendly, that nice, that open, and still be sincere in everything he said. But Kyle was. The first time I really got to know [Kyle] was at ballroom [dance] team tryouts freshman year. He was by far the best dancer trying out, but couldn't stop complimenting people on how well they danced . . . he would never even think about his own tryout. (30)

Kyle was tall, I commented often to him. We sat together for a whole soccer season, continually reassuring each other that our height would get us on the field. Neither of us did [get there,] but it never stopped his smile. Every Day. Every Day. Every Day. Always fun, always radiant, always loved. Always. (31)

IV. Kyle as a Friend

Kyle taught me how to try harder and do everything better. And he showed me how to laugh at my failures and try again. But most of all, Kyle taught me how to be a good man. (32)

Kyle's friendship has meant so much to me these past few years, especially since he took the time to keep it up during school (and tons of extra-curriculars) with emails full of book recommendations and long words that needed a dictionary to be explained. Every person in my family has a specific memory of Kyle that brings laughter and an insight into his personality—like the time he danced the rumba with my sister in our kitchen, or when he yelled for my other sister across the entire college dining hall, with a huge wave and a smile. Kyle brought joy wherever he went because he completely gave of himself to everyone. (33)

Kyle made Harwood dormitory home for many of us. He made any place he went come alive—with faith, passion, or humor. Even for those who did not know him well, Kyle was a source of energy. He had a way of smiling at all of us that told us we were special. It takes a remarkable person to share that kind of joy. (34)

My most vivid memory of Kyle is the dinner we shared on the Friday spring break began, a week before he died. My other friends had already eaten and, although he was fasting for Lent, Kyle insisted on coming with me to the dining hall just so that I wouldn't have to eat alone . . . [T]hat dinner exemplifies the extraordinary selflessness and compassion that distinguished Kyle from the rest of us. (35)

When I hung out with Kyle away from soccer, the glimpse of madness that I saw on the field was complemented by his wild monologues. I won't repeat the stories of his high school soccer days (colored by red cards and punches, I gather) or the tales of his average weekday adventures. Our more philosophical discussions were equally colorful. Each attempt to question his political and religious beliefs met with such a wonderful argument - one that left me agitated, frustrated, smiling, and just plain fascinated. Fascination, come to think of it, is probably the best word I can find to describe my feelings toward Kyle. I was fascinated by his little heel drag of the soccer ball, fascinated by his ability to stand apart from and at the center of any group of people, fascinated by his faith in God, and, most of all, fascinated by his faith in himself. (36)

Kyle has completely altered the way in which I not only view true beauty in such an individual, but also what truly matters in the short lives that we all live. Everything truthful that [Kyle] stood for is exactly what I want to be a part of. I believe that if [Kyle] changed my perception of life, as [he] surely did, then [he] also has affected the hearts of every person whose life has touched his. (38)

My childhood is speckled with memories of Kyle. My favorite is from the summer [his] entire family came up north with my family. We all decided to go on a boat ride together and Kyle, of course, brought a book along for the ride (in almost every memory I have of him, he has a book in his hand). But it wasn't a book that just any nine-year-old would read, it was the largest book I had ever seen besides the Bible. It was a book out of the Tarzan series. He read the entire series during that vacation. I remember the sheer awe I had of him. I wanted to read like him; I wanted to love words as deeply as he did. I still envy that passion. (52)

Every day is a new chance to live my life as fearlessly and as passionately as Kyle did. (39)

From the moment I met [Kyle], I knew I would never be the same. That's how special Kyle was and how genuinely he related to everyone he met. He was so full of life, of goodness, of God, of truth, of light. . . . Kyle squished so much life into his short time on earth. Maybe he was too much for us. Maybe he's needed elsewhere. I know his life and his spirit could never be truly lost. Gone, maybe, not her . . . but never lost. (40)

Whenever I came into contact with [Kyle] I felt loved. You could just tell that he cared for you . . . Kyle had so many characteristics that I'm striving to attain (but for him came naturally). He held such a deep love for life, people, and his faith. . . . (41)

There are two things that I think caused Kyle some anxiety or disappointment at college. One would be girls, and the other would be drinking. As [everyone knew], Kyle was always on the lookout for the mother of his twelve children. I think that he was disappointed by the selection at Pomona because so few of the people there shared his values. Then there was the drinking. I think Kyle was at times upset that so many social activities involved the consumption of large quantities of alcohol. He was a very likable guy so he managed to do very well socially without drinking, but in his heart I believe he wished that others would not drink so much, and that there was more to do on campus than hang out with drunk people. (3)

Kyle was without a doubt the most kind-hearted person I have ever met. Believe me, he did stand out. [His father asked] about how Kyle fi t in while people were drinking. This year, Kyle found an old jacket with "Coors Lite" on the back. The combination of that jacket and his outgoing nature led someone to ask me once if Kyle was a drunk! (42)

When I first met Kyle, I didn't like him. However, by the time I got to know him, he had won me over just like every other person he'd ever met. We were more acquaintances than friends, but from that distance I was able to see how he treated his friends, and it was always with the greatest love and respect. I knew that I could count on him to be good to my friends. I never thanked him for that peace of mind. He was a bright part of my life here, and will remain a bright part of my life wherever I go. (43)

Kyle was one of those people you would see once a day in passing but, through his personality, would make you happier even in momentary contact. He had a way of not only seeing the glass half full himself, but helping me see it as well. Without taking a moral high horse, Kyle was able

 to take the moral high ground. By doing so, he was one of the people I not only respect but . . . could emulate. (44)

[Kyle] was just so much good, and knowing him made my experience here that much better. He never failed to brighten my day each and every time I saw him. Even saying hello to him and having a ten-second conversation with him left me grinning from ear to ear. (30)

I don't think I ever once saw Kyle when he didn't put a smile on my face nearly as big as the one he always had. (46)

I cannot begin to tell you what your son meant to me. I thank God every day that he was a part of my life and that he taught me everything that he did. He inspired me when he was with us, and he continues to inspire me every day. I work harder and play harder than before because I know that would be how Kyle would have wanted me to live. (47)

I know that Kyle was unaware of how much he changed my life at [school] for the better and I am fairly certain the he did not know how much or how fondly I remember him. But I also know that that is just how Kyle was; he always left a greater impression with people than he realized. (50)

I wish you could have been with us Sunday, when Kyle's fellow students in Group 5/Act Five of <u>The Tempest</u> performed in front of Walker Wall. The entire wall was painted with tributes to Kyle, and bestrewn with flowers. In huge letters: "Good night, sweet prince/ And flights of angels sing thee to thy rest." And: "In loving memory of Kyle Maginnis." And many other touching phrases: "Our king of smiles!" I wept through the entire performance, but I smiled too: How happy and proud Kyle would have been of his friends! I felt his presence among us; we all did. Our blessed, beautiful Kyle. (62)

C. Funeral Mass Eulogy by Alvaro DiVicente

March 29, 2003

It's been impressive and surprising to see the number of people this last week who have been touched by Kyle's death, actually who had been touched by his life, but became really apparent by his death.

On Monday, Vytas and Marcelle said that they wanted flowers. And by Wednesday, York Flowers—the flower shop down the street—said they had never seen so much business in their corporate history. So many requests for flowers to be sent to one location.

I called the funeral home to get those cards with Kyle's picture on it and I asked them what would be a good number to order and they said 2000 should be plenty. So I ordered them. Whenever I told people that I ordered 2000, I got some looks and comments like "Really? That's not going to be enough" So we got another thousand and they are going very fast.

Kyle loved life. He was really a volcano of life and love that erupted continuously into that big smile of his. And the smile was his natural look. Looking at the pictures of Kyle these last couple of days, you know they had either a smile or some goofy face where he was making someone else smile. His happiness was contagious, it was infectious. He came into a room, you felt happy. He'd start a conversation. It would be a cheerful conversation. He indeed loved life and had a life full of love. At the same time, Kyle was not quite at home here in the world. He couldn't grasp the concept of time. I remember back in his freshman year, talking with him once, it must have been October.

It was about something we had to do and I said "Kyle, we'll do that in February". And he looked at me with this puzzled face and said, "When is February?" And I said, "It's that short month between January and March, you know, when the days are cloudy and dark." But he looked at me at the end of the conversation and said "Oh, thank you." I then realized that either he truly had no clue of the months or he was a great fake. And I realized that months were not his forte, nor were hours, weeks, days. It was all very blurry to him.

It was most amusing to go on trips with him. His packing had nothing to do with the duration of his trip or the destination. He'd throw something in a bag and be ready to go in 10 minutes. Two things you could be sure of — insufficient clothing and a pair of red soccer shorts. Some of you saw pictures at the wake when he was meeting the pope. If you look carefully, you can only see him from the waist up and you've got to wonder what's on below.

Kyle really didn't fear death. There was the time with the car accident when I know his parents got really upset, everybody did, because he kept saying how he was driving this car at 70 MPH and couldn't understand that he had to slow down on an exit ramp and how he flew off the side of the ramp and almost got himself killed. I remember being very upset with him when I tried to explain to him what could have happened, but death was a foreign concept to him. Either he didn't realize it—or he really didn't care. He saw it as one small step on the way to eternal life.

He had a great sense of mission. He wanted to help people; to serve. Just as he did not care about material possessions, he cared about ideals. He was quite an idealist. He and I were talking last summer a bit about, after he graduated from Pomona, how he would maybe teach at The Heights. And he was really excited. There is so much he could have taught. You know it could have been literature, history, perhaps some Latin, perhaps religion, even math or science. Who knows? Maybe a speed reading course, debate, soccer, ballroom dancing, chess, you name it. He was gifted in all those things and knew them very well. Now we know that the school has lost a very good potential teacher, but you know we have gained an intercessor and all in all we have both come out ahead.

He was searching for his vocation. He was open to the priesthood. He thought about becoming a member of Opus Dei, perhaps a numerary or supernumerary, about getting married. He could have done all those things very, very well. He was uniquely qualified to live all those vocations very well. But at the same, I think now we realize that his vocation was to be Kyle; to be himself. That even though he was searching, he had already found his vocation. And that vocation was followed with extreme generosity.

His vocation showed itself at the time of his confirmation when he chose Tarsicius as his confirmation saint. And Vytas also wanted Tarsicius, but he was a few minutes late. But Kyle chose Tarsicius. Tarsicius was a young boy in the 1st century who was bringing the Eucharist to the martyrs. He was confronted by a pack of thugs who asked him what he was carrying. And Tarsicius realized that these people would not understand why he was carrying the Eucharist and so he did not answer them. They beat him to death with clubs and stones and when they turned the body over there was no trace of the Eucharist. He had either consumed it or it had miraculously disappeared. Kyle was Tarsicius. His mission was to bring Christ to those around him, and he did so very well.

I remember driving down 270 with the school's soccer team after a game, and all of a sudden things got very, very quiet in the back. I listened intently and then realized that they were praying the Rosary. Kyle decided it was time to pray the Rosary and got the whole team doing it. And you've got to wonder, whether they won or lost, how many other teams were praying the Rosary on their way home, because one of the boys had decided to pray the Rosary.

I also remember his senior year we had a soccer tournament at St. Mary's College. It was one of those tournaments where you get there on a Thursday evening and then Friday we'd have two games beginning at 9AM. We found out there was this church that had a 6 o'clock Mass. So Kyle was the one who came over and said, "Do you think we could go to Mass tomorrow?" And I said, "Yeah, I'm sure we could, we'll just have to get up at 5:30, but other than that it's no problem." So he and a few others got up and went to Mass at 6, came back had breakfast and went to the tournament. [They did very well that first game . . . some of you will remember it too.] We would have about two or three hours between games and there was this hill where we would rest and where we could watch some of the other games going on. And it was Kyle's idea to pull out copies of St. Josemaria's *The Way*. We all sat around and there was a bunch of us reading *The Way*. We started a time of prayer with our uniforms on, cleats and sandals. It was this beautiful fall day and the sun was out, and looking around, I realized how good this moment was. You have a bunch of guys who are following the lead of this one senior, Kyle, who is leading them all in a time of prayer. He loved his friends and wanted his friends to be saints. But he was such a natural bearer of Christ: firm, attractive. And now he can really help us, unrestricted by time and by space.

He had a deep love for his family. He truly loved his family. I remember when . . . Marcelle [was] sick in the hospital. . . . In those days Kyle did just about everything for you, Marcelle. Small sacrifices, delaying a glass of water, eating something he didn't want to eat, studying, getting up on time. He did all those things for you. If he went to Mass, he offered it for you. If he prayed the Rosary, the Rosary was for you. If he prayed the Angelus it was for you. You were constantly in his thoughts and in his prayers. And now you know that whatever you want he's going to get it for you.

Vytas, you were his guardian angel. You helped him navigate this world that was too foreign to him, a world that he didn't quite know how to get around in. You protected him so that he could spread love and smiles on everyone wherever he went. You know that Kyle was always immune to peer pressure. He really didn't care what others thought. He never cared what he wore or what he said. He couldn't care less, because he was unfazed by peer pressure. But he had one peer he truly admired and looked up to, and that was you. He really loved you. But even as many wanted to be like Kyle, he wanted to be like you. He always thought (for some reason, I don't know why) you were the coolest, and that was before you got the motorcycle. He was so proud of you, and you know that now he's up in heaven with the angels, telling them great stories. You know his stories—fact and fiction (a bit of a battle) with more fiction than fact. So you'd better get ready because by the time you get up there, there are going to be a lot of stories about you.

Joan and Jack, all of us in this Church and so many others, owe you our most sincere gratitude. Thank you for bringing Kyle into the world. Thank you for raising him and thank you for sharing him with us for however long God allowed us. Twenty years is a very, very short time, but given the fact that he was a true gift, can we complain if we only had him for twenty years? Every praise that you hear of Kyle, is a compliment to you, to the way you raised him. And I know there are no secret formulas for how you raised Kyle, but you had the only one that matters, your unconditional love. He knew he was loved no matter what; that you truly loved him and that was the only thing that mattered. And your love formed him into a true man of God. Kyle will bless you for the rest of your lives. His success is your success. It is unnatural for parents to bury their son, but it is beautiful for parents to have a son in heaven.

Kyle was indeed deeply in love with God, You could not drive in front of a church without Kyle asking "Do you mind if we say the spiritual communion?" And I'd say, "Fine, Kyle, if you want to do that." It was natural. The way he attended Holy Mass, his life of prayer, his love for the

Sacrament of Confession, his devotion to the holy Rosary. He was truly a man in love with God.

A few months ago, some of us in the school got together to come up with what would be a great definition of the ideal Heights student. We came up with the phrase which is written on the poster with some of the pictures of Kyle you saw yesterday: "The glory of God is a man fully alive, doing ordinary things extraordinarily well." And now when I think about Kyle, I realize that what we were doing was really defining him as the ideal Heights student. Those of you who have a card, with Kyle's picture and the poem on the back, may see there on the bottom that it has "Crescite" the motto of the school in Latin. And it is important that that motto is there because that motto is always on the bottom of our shield, holding the shield up. The shield of the school represents everything that is noble and good about the school. And so it is fitting that that motto is at the bottom of the picture of Kyle, because he has truly become a shield of the school, someone that we can strive to imitate.

I know that most of you are already praying to Kyle. I am too. And I think I have figured out how to reach him: You see, Kyle would do anything on a dare. So all you have to do is dare him. Tell him, "Kyle, I'll bet you can't handle this one . . . there is no way you can do this" and he'll get you through. It will work every time. That's what I plan to do when I'm in need. So as we grieve for him we also know he is looking down from heaven—perhaps with a pair of red soccer shorts on—smiling with that smile of his, because he had twenty great years and a great family with many friends, and because he was able to love a lot of people. I know he is up in heaven. All in all, it's not a bad deal for him at all. Kyle, I'll bet you can't get us all up there!

D. Article by Daniel Driscoll (Pomona '05)

The following article was published in Pomona College Student Paper in March 2003.

It is rare to become best friends with someone who's every other opinion is the polar opposite of your own, but then again, Kyle Maginnis was as rare as they come.

I first met Kyle, who died Sunday, March 23, and his twin brother Vytas nearly ten years ago; I encountered the pair six or seven years after that, and then finally once more two years ago. That first time I met the Maginnis twins, when we were all about seven or eight years old, I made the mistake of getting in a dispute with one of them. Though our versions of the story differ—Kyle and Vytas claiming this never happened, I maintaining that it did, and I of course being right—this argument evolved into a bit of a scrap. As I recall, I had managed to pin Kyle or Vytas (in those early years I could never tell the two apart despite their fraternal nature) and was hitting him in the face when, out of nowhere, I felt a blow to my head and suddenly I was being tossed into the side of a soccer goal post. I never figured out with whom I had started that fight, but one thing is certain: It was most certainly the other Maginnis boy who ended it.

Needless to say, I avoided the Maginnis twins for the next several years, but it was inevitable our paths would cross again. I was invited to be a "guest player" for Kyle and Vytas's soccer team at a couple tournaments a year or two before we all started high school. I remember one instance during a game in which a player delivered a series of rather dirty tackles to Vytas's ankles. Although the referee whistled a foul on each of these, Kyle was apparently still not satisfied.

So when that player jumped in the air to head the ball, Kyle—with a running start from his sweeper position—delivered a hit that resembled one of those ice hockey checks that sends a guy spiraling through the air. However, Kyle, with his trademark "Kyle's ball!" scream, somehow managed to get a piece of his head on the leather sphere as well and the ref never blew his whistle. There was no way Kyle was going to allow a hit on his brother to go unpunished, but even more, he was clever enough to get his vengeance in a way that still played by the rules.

For the most part, I didn't see the Maginnis kids for most of my high school years, the exception being one soccer game between their school and my own in which Kyle dove and made a game-saving one-handed stop on the line to protect a tie (the fact that Kyle was technically not the goalkeeper was of little consequence to him, and to the great displeasure of my team, it didn't occur to the ref either).

Indeed, it wasn't until the day of my high school graduation that the Maginnis boys would become my friends for good. Though I had never known it, I had in fact passed the Maginnis house several times each day, and it was just five minutes from my own. So it was that as I drove by one day, I noticed someone running after my car, and when I reached the stop sign at the end of the block, that person tapped on my window.

"Hey!" said the smiling stranger.

There was an awkward pause for a moment, and I wondered aloud whether I might have left a coffee cup on my roof.

"No, it's your bumper sticker. I'm going to Pomona next year."

We talked a bit after that and traded phone numbers. Of course, when Kyle called around 7:30 the following morning to see if I wanted to go to a movie that evening, I wondered who this kid was and what I had gotten myself into. As I would discover, hanging out with Kyle, Vytas, and all of their friends brought me into a world in which friendships were based on loyalty and good deeds rather than pretensions and peer-pressure. Indeed, if it hadn't been for Kyle's tap on my window, I may never have gotten to know some of my closest friends today.

As luck would have it, Kyle and I were both planning to play soccer for Pomona-Pitzer that year, and so we agreed that we should train with each other that summer. By the time August rolled around, we had been fairly good about training six days a week, and in the process we played with groups ranging from over-the-hillers to high school kids to college players, not to mention one game with a pair of MLS starters. When a letter came in the mail from Coach Swartz that we needed to be able to do 200-straight pushups, I was in disbelief. Kyle, on the other hand, simply gave me one of his famously goofy grins, and said that anyone with a good plan can accomplish anything. I think I cut him off when he started into a Biblical passage that would serve as inspiration, but I admired his confidence and believed in him. Sure enough, when tryouts rolled around, for the first time in my life I managed to do 200 straight pushups next to Kyle's 225. We were both disappointed by the fact that Coach Swartz never carried out his threat of testing us that season, but being able to prove the achievement to ourselves may have been an even greater reward. That experience helped explain why Kyle thought graduating Summa Cum Laude was a very achievable goal. He honestly believed that everything was in his reach.

In little over a year and a half at Pomona College, Kyle established himself as one of the most diversely talented members of the student body. In addition to playing on the soccer team his freshman year, he was one of just a few first-year students selected to compete on the Claremont Colleges' ballroom team which last year won the national championship. This year, he was honored to be named a Writing Fellow. Just last fall, he appeared on the television trivia show *WinTuition* and won thousands of dollars in prizes. Even with so many varied activities, Kyle still managed to be named a Distinguished Scholar while attending Mass daily at Claremont's Our Lady of the Assumption Church.

It was not until the end of our freshman year that Kyle began to make sense to me. For a long time, his deep religious convictions and unflexing Catholic principles would perplex me (despite my own background at a Catholic high school, Kyle is the only kid I have ever met who tried to debate religious philosophy on bus rides to-and-from soccer games), and at times I wondered if he was too zealous to be taken seriously. Sometimes I wondered if Kyle was self-centered, for he was almost never on time for anything and there were times when he didn't seem to respect other people's belongings, for so many things he "borrowed"—the quotation marks being necessary because he didn't always ask permission when he used other people's things—ended up broken. Despite all that, I never once grew mad at him, and which made the least sense to me of all.

Near the end of that freshman year, I was at dinner with Kyle and a large group of people, and as I sat quietly at the table, I had an epiphany of sorts. Suddenly, my unusual friend made perfect sense.

First, while for many religion is a weekend hobby whose symbols people boast with just a little more pride than one has for their favorite team, for Kyle, one's faith was not only a definition of how to live life, it was one's life. Kyle loved God so much that he considered becoming a priest or a numerary (though he also mentioned wanting a family with 12 kids, so clearly there was a conflict of interest). Sure, he knew temptation like everyone else, but unlike everyone else, Kyle's faith in God was so strong that his faith in himself was able to withstand the inevitable pressures that a secular world provides against a Christian life. Kyle wasn't zealous, he was just in love. With God, life, and all the possibilities in between.

Kyle wasn't self-centered, and he wasn't careless either. He was just oblivious. The reason he was late for everything was because he was always so busy doing so many things, and on top of those things he always tried to make room for one more job, hobby, or friend. It was impossible to juggle everything perfectly, but Kyle was determined to try, even if the cycle lost its shape every so often. As for his borrowing habits, from the bikes he broke to the movies and books he lost, not to mention the food— considering he was a Writing Fellow, I never did comprehend how Kyle believed that one could digest another's food and still call it "borrowing"— the great irony was that Kyle actually made every effort to keep track of things that he borrowed and return them as they were. The problem was, for all his talents, keeping track of stuff and not breaking it was Kyle's Achilles' heel. With that in mind, it suddenly made sense why, after the most painful experience of my Pomona career—riding a bike that Kyle had used the day before up a hill, having the seat fall off without my noticing, then sitting back down quickly, etc.—I still couldn't get upset at him when he told me "Oh yeah, I think I broke the seat yesterday. Sorry I forgot to mention it." A common joke while riding with Kyle was "Kyle, stop sign!" He would always ask "Where?," to which I would respond "10 yards back!" In the last few days, even that made sense to me. He never said anything about being color-blind, but considering Kyle wanted to be friends with everyone no matter how different or difficult they could be, it makes sense that a person who didn't focus on the red in one's personality probably couldn't see the red in a stop sign either.

This past summer, Kyle and Vytas made a trip to our friend's beach house. To Vytas's great chagrin, Kyle realized during the 3-hour drive out that he had made plans to go bowling the next evening and insisted that he couldn't cancel. Since Kyle's parents had taken him off their car insurance a few months earlier, Vytas would be forced to drive Kyle home. We all thought this was crazy, but while Kyle may not have been good about being on time, he always made sure to get there eventually. Even if it was just to go bowling. That didn't give the brothers too much time to stay at the beach, but it was still enough Kyle to deliver one of his most memorable lines.

Shortly before Kyle and Vytas planned to drive back home, our host's new girlfriend came by unannounced and sat in a chair next to Kyle. True to his usual form, Kyle peppered the hungover girl with a barrage of inquiries that included serious questions about what she wanted to do with her life (the girl was 17) and how she perceived God, as well as what her lucky number was and did she ever read Spot Goes to School as a kid. The confused girl excused herself and left in the middle of all this with the impression that Kyle was gay and in a cult. As the girl walked out the gate, Kyle turned to my brother and, in his best effort at a whisper, announced to anyone in a 2 mile radius, "Man, that girl was really awkward!"

No Kyle, you were really awkward. And that's why we loved you. Because in a world that tends to highlight the worst elements in life, you were one of those unusual people who always found a reason to bring out a big goofy smile.

From you, so many others and I learned to smile too.

E. Article by Pam Noles, Los Angeles Times

April 26, 2003 Student's Death Leaves 'Huge Hole'

Pomona College's Kyle Maginnis, 20, is remembered as a talented, selfless person who made a difference in the lives of those around him.

Pam Noles, Inland Valley Voice

CLAREMONT — Kyle Maginnis could be a little absent-minded, misplacing borrowed CDs and bicycles with equal ease, to the bafflement of others. His entire family once raced through an airport begging reservation clerks for help because Kyle forgot the airline, flight number, departure time and routing destinations that were to get him home from a Christmas break in Washington, D.C., back to Pomona College.

And yet his mind was brilliant. His writing ability got him nominated as a Fellow at his college and tapped to help other students with anything from writing a term paper to filling out a grad school application. He was also keen with math, using those skills to enhance his already prodigious abilities playing pool, a skill taught to him by his father that he could have honed into a professional career, had he chosen that path.

He didn't. He wanted to be a high school teacher. He wanted a family. He was a warm and funny 20-year-old who shunned automatic membership into the post-irony generation. What's more, sarcasm just didn't register for him. He communicated through sincerity, not snarky shorthand.

Above all, Kyle Maginnis loved God. He did not evangelize his faith, he lived it with full joy, his knowledge of the truth of the hereafter so unshakable that his attorney parents overcame initial reservations about sending him to a secular college. They figured their son's world view, framed by his Catholic upbringing, could do the other students a world of good.

When Kyle died unexpectedly March 23, just two days after walking into a hospital complaining of headaches, dizziness and balance problems, the devastation ripped through the Claremont Colleges, touching students, professors and administrators.

"He knew everybody. He didn't really believe in limiting himself," said friend Dan Driscoll. "He came to Pomona, which is about as secular as they come, with an open heart, even though he got into Notre Dame. He was known for being entirely unpretentious, unassuming. He was so genuine you couldn't help but to fall for him, in a way. Even though, I'm telling you, every other opinion you just didn't agree with."

A memorial for Kyle will be held at 3 p.m. Monday at Bridges Hall of Music, with a reception to follow at Carolyn Lyon Garden. His parents, Jack and Joan Maginnis, his fraternal twin, Vytas, and 15-year-old sister, Marcelle, will be guests at the ceremony.

Kyle loved a good debate, lived for it, his debating skills honed while growing up in a home with no television and parents who believed in healthy discussion.

Pomona College soccer coach Bill Swartz, for whom Kyle played defender during the 2001-2002 season, sparred with Kyle on bus trips. As his religious and academic commitments grew this academic year, Kyle stepped off the field but still helped out with videotaping games, offering moral support to the team. He maintained his relationships with team members even after he stopped playing full time. He would stop by the office to chat and once, seeing Swartz in the cafeteria, Kyle walked over just to ask how his former coach's day was going.

"Kyle was unique," Swartz said. "He affected all of us, always had a smile."

The college's ballroom dance coach, Wes Acker, said Kyle's "infectious smile" and open demeanor made him a good performer. Kyle loved doing the lifts and he liked to play dance jokes, pulling fabulous moves in practice that were, of course, illegal in competition.

"I don't know anybody who didn't like him," Acker said. "He was gregarious and kind of mischievous, in a nice way."

When Neil Gerard, associate dean of students, hired Kyle to teach a recreational pool course at the Smith Campus Center, "he was all over it," Gerard said. "He was very patient with them [his students], very thorough."

These stories of generosity and faith do not surprise his parents.

"I'd love to take credit for it but the kid was sort of born with an open heart," said Jack Maginnis. "All we can claim credit for is not spoiling him."

It wasn't easy for his son to become so beloved, he said. During his first year at Pomona, Kyle shared how he was having difficulty getting his peers to accept that he was a young man of deep faith but also a peer who was not sitting in judgment of them. He had a hard time fitting in, seeming "like an alien creature to them at first," his father said. Kyle continued being himself, putting himself out there, until people accepted him.

"He had a very real love for God and he loved people, everybody, kind of like God loves people, indiscriminately," Jack Maginnis said. "He would just bug them until he understood them. It was always a welcome annoyance to anyone who encountered him because it was so warm."

Kyle had a schedule for his life, his father said, and was worried that he was falling a bit behind. According to his plan, by this point he should have met his future bride and been preparing for the family phase of his life. He wanted a large family. However, he told his father, he was having a bit of trouble on the dating front.

It wasn't until after his death, while visiting campus and meeting some of his son's friends, that his father realized what was going on.

"It wasn't until a visited Pomona that I saw the difficulty," Jack Maginnis said. "He was telling people he wanted 12 children!"

Maginnis was expecting to meet maybe a few of his son's friends while on campus in the days immediately after Kyle's death. Instead, 250 showed up for an impromptu sharing at the dorm. In retrospect, he shouldn't have been surprised he said; at Kyle's wake and funeral mass in St. Mary Mother of God in Washington, more than 1,000 people turned out.

These were not just friends of his parents, but Kyle's peers, teachers, friends and others touched by him.

Kyle had a fun side, too. He auditioned for and landed a spot on the now defunct Comedy Central show "Win Tuition," where he won a bit of money, some camping gear and other prizes. His chronic lateness — Kyle's desire to be of help far outstripped the number of hours in a day — somehow came across as more endearing than irritating.

Beverly Wilson Palmer, coordinator of the writing program for the college, said Kyle had a deft touch when working with students in the throes of a writing crisis.

"He was a very breezy person. Most of the students around here, they're afraid to show enthusiasm, they're afraid to show how much they care," Palmer said. "He wasn't. He was genuinely enthusiastic."

Kyle instituted new procedures, such as having those tutored write critiques of their tutors. Far from being afraid of the potential of such honest criticism, Kyle saw how it could help the tutors spot areas in their own performance that needed improvement, thus raising the quality of help offered the students.

His critiques were filled with praise over his ability to help others feel confident of their projects and their ability to complete them and to deepen their understanding of the writing process.

"I had a feeling he was going to make a mark on this world," Palmer said. "I felt he would be one. He's left a huge hole here."

The void left in his family is also vast.

Joan Maginnis has a favorite photograph of Kyle, taken when he was about 10. He sits on the rooftop of a partially built home, smiling down at the photographer. The sun shines behind him so brightly, his image is half vanished.

"He's there, and not there, at the same time laughing, one foot in eternity," she wrote in an e-mail. "He loved God more than life, the Giver more than the gift. That's what set him so apart."

Friends back home in Washington have told his parents they are already calling on Kyle in his new role in heaven. In the Catholic faith, followers may ask those gone on to heaven to intercede on their behalf.

"They are satisfied beyond any doubt that Kyle is in heaven and they are asking for intercessions from him in their prayers," his father said. "There are friends of ours certain of Kyle's saintliness. We agree, and we say he's still our son and he has to do what we say."

F. March 13, 2003 Reference Letter by Professor Martha Andresen In Support of Kyle's Application to the Notre Dame Traditio Seminar

Dear Colleagues:

I am pleased to write on behalf of Kyle Maginnis, who is an applicant to your 2003 Traditio Summer Seminar Program. Kyle is a sophomore at Pomona College who enrolled Fall term 2002 in my class, Shakespeare: Comedies and Histories, and who is currently enrolled (Spring term 2003) in a second class, Shakespeare: Tragedies and Romances. Last fall, in a large class (50 students) Kyle was my top student (receiving an A+); this spring he promises to repeat this performance in an equally large class. In my office, on many delightful occasions, Kyle and I have spoken at length about Shakespeare, about other mutual literary interests, about his profound religious conviction, observances, and activism, and, above all, about dimensions of his vital spiritual life, defined by a lifetime quest to study, explore, practice, and develop his faith. Kyle has indicated to me that he wishes to enroll this summer in your intriguing and inspired seminar, "Reconciling Heart and Mind." I wish to affirm here that I cannot imagine a student more perfectly qualified, given Kyle's superlative intellectual, academic and spiritual gifts, nor can I envision a young Christian in greater need of such intensive and sustaining inquiry. Kyle will give to this seminar as much as he will gain: he is uniquely generous, and he will be uniquely receptive, enriched, and possibly transformed by the experience.

In my view, Kyle's astonishing distinctiveness is his life's blessing and burden: this most gregarious, energetic, generous, warm, and endearing young man, by virtue of his unique brilliance, his emotional intensity, his unequalled drive, discipline, and spiritual zeal, stands alone. The exceptional gifts that have won him unmatched distinction, demonstrated in a dazzling array of activities and honors, including (among many others) debate, ballroom dancing, soccer, tutoring, Christian leadership—in addition to his stellar academic achievement—make him a rarity even among his diversely talented and high achieving cohort at Pomona College. Among the thousands of students I have taught during thirty years at Pomona, Kyle is in a class by himself, by virtue of incandescent energies of mind ~ spirit. I have never encountered a student for whom

Christianity is studied and practiced with greater sophistication and passion. I have never encountered a student who has embraced Shakespeare—and each and every subject he undertakes—with greater sophistication and passion: Kyle's essays for me, one on Shylock, and another on Desdemona and Othello, are masterpieces of originality, intensity, subtlety, care, and eloquence, of publishable quality. More: Kyle is an immensely talented Shakespearean actor. He stole the show in a hilarious performance of Petruchio last fall, and no doubt he will do so again, this spring, in his performance of Prospero, a role brilliantly suited to his precocious wisdom and "old soul." All that Kyle embraces he masters with exuberance and excellence. His professors and his fellow students alike simply marvel. Yet "standing alone" has fueled Kyle's most profound emotional and spiritual searching: he yearns for kindred souls, for a community of Christians who seek, within the frenzy of secular academic and professional achievement, a core of connection to divine presence and to values that profoundly center, nurture, and transcend the acclaim—and the isolation—that public distinction can confer.

Kyle is the child of Christian optimism in a suffering world. He has known and felt many sorrows. Such sorrows have indeed carved out and shaped this young man's "old soul," deepening his uncanny awareness, empathy, and compassion, driving his own will to mastery and achievement, humbling his spirit and directing his faith. Kyle's "pride in achievement" is never arrogance; it is wonder and gratitude. He found a way to achieve and survive; now he seeks ways to thrive. We have conversed about this crucial distinction on many occasions: for Kyle, thriving means life in the spirit, and life in a community, founded on clarity of values, affirmation of faith, practice of worship and service, and giving of gifts, efforts that must underpin all else, however abundantly the secular world praises his achievements or rewards him with honors and positions of leadership. Kyle seeks to lead, he seeks to teach, and no young person I know is better qualified to do so. But he cannot do so without resolving the deeper conflicts and issues attendant on reconciling demands of world and soul, mind and heart, public ambition and acclaim, and private healing and wholeness.

For these reasons, and many more, your Traditio summer program is perfectly suited for Kyle Maginnis, and he, in turn, is perfectly qualified for it. This brilliant and passionate young man has, therefore, my most confident, enthusiastic, and affectionate recommendation.

Sincerely,

Martha Andresen
Phebe Estelle Spalding
Professor of English

G. April 28, 2003 Pomona Memorial Service Address

by Richard Cannon

Kyle Maginnis was known for many things all around the five colleges. He was first and foremost an academic, but also an amazing ballroom dancer, a dedicated soccer player, the five college undisputed pool champion, a writing fellow, an emerging thespian, and the list goes on and on. Kyle excelled at everything he set his mind to and most of us know how busy Kyle's mind was.

I will always remember Kyle and his marvelous qualities. Continual optimism. A fellow soccer player of ours described it best: "Kyle was one of those people you would see once a day in passing but, through his personality, he would make you happier even in momentary contact. He had a way of not only seeing the glass half full himself but helping others see it as well." It was true; Kyle's optimism was contagious. I can vividly remember how easy it was for him to cheer our friends up. As many of you know, Kyle's fellow suitemates and I are all taking organic chemistry which has very difficult tests every other Friday. So, Kyle being the good friend he was would hunt us down late Thursday night and give us some support . . . or should I say he would find us and tease us endlessly about his absurdly hard half page English response that was due in two weeks. Then the next day after the test at lunch when we suitemates were all discouraged about how poorly the test went, Kyle would say something like "Geez, guys let me tell you about how hard my organic-chem test was this morning. It was so difficult that . . ." As he trailed off because one of the rest of us were throwing our lunches at him. Now, some of you might be saying continual optimism, sounds like continually pestering. But no, not at all. We loved it. It would cheer us up so much just to have him around, no matter how horrible our test had turned out or how late we had stayed up preparing for it. Kyle was always able to brighten the day of those around him merely because he saw such a bright day himself.

Dedication and commitment. Kyle was the pinnacle of dedication. Religion was such a large part of his life that I have never met a more religiously committed individual, which is saying quite a bit considering I grew up in Utah. Kyle's commitment shone through academically as well. I can't even count how many nights I went to sleep watching Kyle type a paper at his computer and then would wake up the next morning and he had apparently not even moved. "Kyle," I would say, "Didn't you get any sleep? I thought your paper only needed to be two pages?" "It did," he would respond as my printer was spouting out page after page of text with so many citations and footnotes that even my high school English teacher would have gagged. That was typical because Kyle always went above and beyond whatever was expected, even if it was only a small task.

Kyle and I would debate the importance of grades all the time, and I'm not a great debater, as he was, but he never believed my side for a moment. I would hypothesize, "Kyle, grades are not everything. Ten years from now you will be able to teach at any high school you want and turning all your hair gray over trying to getting an "A plus", as he would say, is not going to change that." He would retort, "But what about graduate school, and my doctorate, I wouldn't be able to graduate summa cum laude and then I will not get the fellowship I need and, and, and . . ." Kyle's drive to excel and achieve was so natural and deeply rooted that he had no other option but success. No one could have stopped him from becoming the most that he could be.

Athletics was another substantial part of his life, and an area his competitiveness thrived. Kyle would do everything he could to win or be the best at everything. Whether it was a heated Nintendo game, a race of Mario Kart up in the tower where we lived, or an intramural soccer game. One opponent commented that he had always thought Kyle was a really nice guy, until his team played Kyle's in intramural soccer, then Kyle was as intense about winning the intramural quarterfinals match as Mohammed Ali was about the Rumble in the Jungle. Also, anyone who decided to venture into the gym with Kyle knew his intensity. The tall, scrawny Kyle would go over to the rack of 45 lbs. weights and just start loading them onto the bench press. Easy Kyle, that weight could crush a small horse! most would think.

Then the next thing you know he was pushing it up off his chest with the most strained look on his face, and after barely doing it once, he would try to do it again. Usually the person who had accompanied him that was looking forward to a nice leisurely stroll in the gym would then have to pull half the gym's weights up off of Kyle's chest.

Kyle was also a man of the ladies. Now, don't take that in the wrong way. By no means was he a player so to speak, but he loved to have crushes and take dates to the dining hall, and the whole bit. We would stay up late at night talking about what this girl said to him . . . or how this other might like him or how she responded to this situation. Usually to be cut short by our neighbor banging on the wall we share and shouting "Shut up in there."

Finally, and most generally, Kyle loved life. He loved every day that he was alive and would have continued to love the days until he was 327. Every day presented itself with new obstacles and challenges just ready for him to step up and try. I remember a very interesting conversation that Kyle and I had during Spring Break, right before he passed away. We were friendly debating about life in general, and I came up with a great question. Little did I know the importance of what we were lightly discussing. I asked him what he would think of his life if it were finished tomorrow? His response stunned me then and still strikes me as amazing. I have been thinking about this often lately and to feel the way Kyle did is a life goal for many as well as myself. He responded that he would be happy and satisfied with his life. He explained that he had lived life to its fullest, had an absolute love for God, and had so many opportunities and done so many wonderful things that he felt complete contentment with his life. I find that absolutely amazing.

These memories that we all share with Kyle, and his continual optimism, exuberant personality, perpetual happiness, and sheer love of life will live on forever in the people that knew and loved him.

H. A Commendation for Kyle Chrysostom Maginnis

(November 23, 1982—March 23, 2003) Pomona College Class of 2005

Presented on May 14, 2004 by the Gamma Chapter of Pomona College Phi Beta Kappa

The golden key we wear, as recent or long-time members of Phi Beta Kappa, signifies the excellence of mind, character, and achievement honored by the Society in America for more than two hundred years. The Greek letters inscribed on our pin, we are reminded today, signify the motto "Love of wisdom, guide of life," and the image of a finger pointing to three stars signifies "the ambition of young scholars and the three distinguishing principles of the Society: friendship, morality, and learning."

Today, by means of commendation, the Gamma chapter of Pomona College honors a brilliant young scholar who, in his two years among us, personified such excellence, lived according to such principles, and whose ambition for learning and service reached to the stars: Kyle Chrysostom Maginnis. All who knew Kyle knew this: he was the best of students and the kindest of friends; an exemplar of profound faith, practiced values, and perfect integrity. And no person loved wisdom and life more. Kyle's gifts were stellar, and they were precocious; here is a poem he wrote in the seventh grade:

> A treasure trove is life
> A chest of golden chances
> A shining gem, a crown of pearls,
> This is life.
>
> As varied as a silken tapestry
> It is an infinite thing.

On March 23, 2003, while only a sophomore, Kyle died suddenly of a brain aneurysm, leaving us bereft of his radiant presence and his own dreams unfulfilled. One dream dear to Kyle was to be elected to Phi Beta Kappa as a junior. Were he still with us, surely that dream would be a reality, in that by spring term of his sophomore year, Kyle ranked among the top five in his class and showed every promise of maintaining such outstanding academic achievement. Today we wish to recognize posthumously Kyle's magnificence as a scholar and a human being. Therefore, in the presence of all gathered here—especially the new initiates of the class of 2004 and 2005, as well as Kyle's parents, Joan and Jack Maginnis—the Gamma Chapter, by unanimous acclaim, now commends Kyle Chrysostom Maginnis for the excellence of mind and character celebrated and memorialized by Phi Beta Kappa.

CPSIA information can be obtained
at www.ICGtesting.com
Printed in the USA
LVHW072148080223
739072LV00026B/597